The Struggle for Hegemony in Pakistan

'A major analysis of our world's political crisis and a brilliant critique of the ideology of middle-class aspiration.'

—Professor Joel Wainwright, Ohio State University

'Shows how an aspirational idea of the middle class reinforces the subordination of dispossessed labour, ethnic minorities in peripheral territories, terrorists and deviant dissenters. This wide-ranging book is sure to stimulate critical scholarship and organic intellectual activism both inside and outside South Asia.'

—Barbara Harriss-White, Emeritus Professor and Fellow, Wolfson College, University of Oxford

'Akhtar powerfully channels the spirit of Gramsci and Fanon to critique neoliberal hegemony in Pakistan – and to diagnose the next great battlefield for the Afro-Asian Left: the values, aspirations, and solidarities of the digitised youth across core and periphery.'

—Majed Akhter, Senior Lecturer, Department of Geography, King's College London

'Drawing with insight on Gramsci, and located in the Global South, this accomplished book is an important contribution to the search for progressive, anti-colonial, and humanist revolutionary politics in Pakistan and beyond.'

—Professor John Chalcraft, London School of Economics and Political Science

'What is the "political" in Pakistan, and how does this help update our theories on democratic backsliding and contemporary authoritarianism? Why do we want to think of the middle class at the centre of it all again? Read this book to find out.'

—Shandana Mohmand, Research Fellow, Institute of Development Studies, University of Sussex

The Struggle for Hegemony in Pakistan

Fear, Desire and Revolutionary Horizons

Aasim Sajjad Akhtar

PLUTO PRESS

First published 2022 by Pluto Press
New Wing, Somerset House, Strand, London WC2R 1LA

www.plutobooks.com

Extracts published from:

Aasim Sajjad Akhtar and Ammar Rashid (2021) 'Dispossession and the militarised developer state: Financialisation and class power on the agrarian–urban frontier of Islamabad, Pakistan'. *Third World Quarterly* 42 (8) pp. 1866–1884 (reproduced by kind permission of Taylor & Francis)

Aasim Sajjad Akhtar (2022) 'The Checkpost State in Pakistan's War of Terror: Centres, Peripheries, and the Politics of the Universal'. *Antipode* (reproduced by kind permission of John Wiley and Sons)

Aasim Sajjad Akhtar (2021) 'The War of Terror in Praetorian Pakistan: The Emergence and Struggle of the Pashtun Tahaffuz Movement'. *Journal of Contemporary Asia* 51 (3) pp. 516–529 (reproduced by kind permission of Taylor & Francis)

British Library Cataloguing in Publication Data
A catalogue record for this book is available from the British Library

ISBN 978 0 7453 4667 0 Hardback
ISBN 978 0 7453 4666 3 Paperback
ISBN 978 0 7453 4670 0 PDF
ISBN 978 0 7453 4668 7 EPUB

Typeset by Stanford DTP Services, Northampton, England
Printed and bound by CPI Group (UK) Ltd, Croydon, CR0 4YY

Contents

Preface and acknowledgements

My motivation for writing this book is straightforward. In my previous book, *The Politics of Common Sense* (Cambridge, 2018), I deployed a Gramscian framework to elucidate how the pro-imperialist military regime of General Zia ul Haq (1977–1988) designed and executed a ruling-class project hegemonised around a cynical politics of patronage. As was the case with all reactionary regimes around the world at the onset of the neoliberal counter-revolution, the Zia dictatorship sought to suppress the substantial revolutionary currents that had threatened propertied classes and the country's powerful military establishment in the preceding conjuncture.

In more than three decades since General Zia ul Haq's demise, the hegemonic order has been largely insulated from anti-systemic popular class mobilisation. Many students, political companions and academic peers who engaged generously with *The Politics of Common Sense* have at the same time questioned why I did not attend to the imperative of rehabilitating progressive politics and fomenting an alternative hegemonic conception. Put simply: what is to be done?

Even without any coaxing, I have obsessed about this challenge since at least the *coup d'etat* of October 1999 when General Pervez Musharraf became Pakistan's fourth military dictator. I had returned to the country after completing graduate school a year before the coup and became immediately involved with Pakistan's emaciated left. At 22 years young, I was the exception in the ranks, virtually all other comrades hailing from the generation that had lived through the painful defeat of actually existing socialism.

With neoliberal globalisation at its zenith, the old guard was a source of inspiration simply because it resisted the tidal waves of capitalist triumphalism that engulfed Pakistan (and the world at large). Yet, while myself and a handful of other youngsters wanted to immerse ourselves in organic working people's struggles, whatever their shape and form, older comrades' revolutionary imaginaries were often out of sync with our novel organising methods.

Over these past 23 years, I have seen much change in organising circles. Like many on the left in much of the world, we in Pakistan too today take solace in having resuscitated the idea that naming and challenging capitalism and its various affiliated political forms at the global, national and local scales is once again on the agenda.

Our progress is most evident in the fact that a new generation of young people has gravitated towards critical ideas and political action. But in a country that boasts a predominantly young population – approximately 150 million of Pakistan's 230 million people are below the age of 30 – we do not yet constitute a critical mass to penetrate the hegemonic mainstream. Young progressives are certainly on the frontlines of movements of resistance – to imperialist war, state repression, class/caste exploitation, dispossession, patriarchal norms and violence, climate change, privatisation of public services, and so much more – but a theory of revolutionary politics that can appeal to the majority of Pakistan's people in the medium and long run remains conspicuous by its absence. In fact, as I argue in this book, most of Pakistan's young people are imbued with a hegemonic middle-class aspiration.

Put differently, the rebuilding/resuscitating of left discourse/politics has not necessarily translated into a viable imaginary *sufficient* for a hegemonic political project, a Gramscian national-popular collective will, as it were. It is noteworthy that few amongst today's young progressives identify themselves as 'revolutionaries' in the mould of the past, and they are more likely to be active on Facebook and Twitter than physically seeking out and working with the proverbial worker and peasant. Under the backdrop of what I call an increasingly digitalised lifeworld, the meaning and practice of progressive politics is changing even more rapidly than ever.

As such, this book attempts to achieve two separate but interrelated goals. First, I present an empirical and theoretical sketch of actually existing capitalism in Pakistan. What forms do globalised finance capitalism take in a highly uneven social formation that continues to bear the legacies of colonialism? What is the class/demographic structure of Pakistani society? How is contemporary hegemony (re)produced in both banal and spectacular ways, especially in the age of the mass/digital media? How are patriarchy, ethnic-national oppression, caste and other forms of identity inscribed onto the patronage-based structure of power?

Second, I offer some building blocks for a theory of politics that can lead us, tentatively, in the direction of what Jodi Dean has named the 'communist horizon'. How do we foment a hegemonic alternative to what I call the politics of fear and desire? Can we do so without deeply interrogating objective changes in the field of politics, and particularly to the digitalisation of this field? How can the burgeoning contradictions of contemporary capitalism – including but not limited to imperialist wars, ecological breakdown and the creation of a mass reserve army of labour/surplus populations – become the basis of an emancipatory collective subject rather than a dramatic race to the bottom based on hate of the proverbial 'other'?

I do not offer answers to all of these questions, only points of departure. In what I understand to be a long(ish) war of position, deeply interrogating the relations of force and attendant problematics of political subjectivity and consciousness that will shape left politics in times to come is, I believe, of primary importance. While I focus on Pakistan, the book offers insights relevant to the postcolonial regions of South Asia and Sub-Saharan Africa more generally.

Ultimately, of course, what our future holds will be determined in the course of struggle. My own struggle has gone through many phases since I started out in the late 1990s. Whatever the ebbs and flows, however, the terrain of active politics has thrown up lifelong relationships. In a society as brutalised as Pakistan's, to continue immersing oneself in popular struggles while sustaining one's own humanity is a task unto itself. The task of transforming society, as Gramsci and many more revolutionaries have always reminded us, goes hand in hand with transforming oneself, and I am grateful to still be waging both my inner fight and the collective struggle with the closest of comrades/friends. To those who have seen me through the most difficult of times – you know who you are.

Some who have become comrades in struggle first became known to me in the classroom and varsity setting. I am thankful to students at my home institution of Quaid-i-Azam University (QAU) in Islamabad from whom I continue to learn much – I am sure many will shape left-progressive horizons in times to come. Beyond the realm of formal politics, it is extremely gratifying to bear witness to a number of former students – both from QAU and the Lahore University of Management Sciences (LUMS) where I taught previously – who have become amazing critical scholars in their own right. I learn at least as much from them now as they ever did from me.

It was during my time away from Pakistan in 2019–2020 that I completed most of the work on this book. I thank the South Asia Institute at SOAS and the Oxford Centre for Islamic Studies for allowing me to be solely an academic for the first time in my adult life.

I was still in the UK when the novel coronavirus took the world by storm, and have not seen my Singaporean side of the family since. In truth, I see little of Ruby, Sajjad, Usman, Emaad, Saba, Esa, Hasan and Hana Noor at the best of times, but the pandemic has engendered separation for far longer than any of us have ever experienced. Like so many others, I too hope that we will soon be able to at least spend those precious few weeks a year together again.

In the meantime, I am immensely lucky to enjoy the daily companionship of Asha and Neil, for however long we get to enjoy it. It is not always easy, but I will remember these times as some of the best of my life. Hajra, Pervez and Sadia regularly offer both wisdom and support, and I hope that I offer a little bit of the same to them too.

I will never take for granted the long journeys that Alia and I have traversed and the hard work that we have put in to get to where we are today. I look forward to what is still ahead of us, and I will continue trying to help you grow and love in something that approximates the way that you have always done for me.

The joy that Bella and Rafay bring to me is hard to explain, even to myself. They are like rays of light that never stop shining. I love you both dearly and am extremely proud to call you my own.

Rumi – my little boy – has grown into a young man that embodies courage, empathy and love on a daily basis. I sometimes still stop and pinch myself that you are who and where you are. As you venture out into the world, always know that Abba will be your biggest supporter. In effect, this book is for you and your siblings who will very soon take on the task of building a world worth living in for future generations too.

To the many more young people in Pakistan and beyond, I present this book as a sobering reminder of the brutalisation spawned by the rule of capital and colonial statecraft, but also as a framework for thinking through the potentialities of creating an alternative and shared future. We can be like ostriches in the sand or align ourselves with the tradition of revolutionary humanism that has for centuries sought to transform our patriarchal, colonised and capitalist world. I have spent most of my life trying to do justice to this revolutionary legacy, and if more of us choose the same path, we can still avert a descent into barbarism.

Aasim Sajjad
Islamabad, October 2021

Introduction

Middle-class hegemonies in theory and history

The emergence of the novel coronavirus and subsequent shutdown of organised economic life in 2020 was described as a 'once-in-a-generation' emergency. In truth, the COVID-19 pandemic simply magnified the scale of the interlocking political, economic, cultural and environmental crises that afflict humankind and nature. Popular movements like Occupy Wall Street and the Arab Spring triggered by the global financial crash of 2006–2008 gestured towards an alternative hegemony to contest the rule of capital. A decade on, the pandemic served as a sober reminder of the untrammelled power of military–industrial–media establishments and political demagogues around the world, exacerbating the contradictions of contemporary capitalism without care of consequence.

Donald Trump's defeat in the US presidential election of November 2020 was hailed by mainstream pundits as a respite for the institutions of liberal democracy in both western countries and the rest of the world. That Trump's successor in the White House, Joe Biden, epitomised the return to 'normalcy' betrays the fact that it was, in fact, the neoliberal normal that produced 'Trump-Bannonism' in the first place.[1]

In August 2021, the Biden administration handed Afghanistan back to the Taliban after 20 years of imperialist bloodletting. The shambolic scenes in Kabul and the rest of the country at the conclusion of the longest war in US history brought into focus how a declining American Empire continues to champion violence and unbridled profiteering to sustain political-economic projects of domination around the globe.

Recall that only three decades ago proclamations of peace and prosperity for all humankind reverberated across the length and breadth of the planet. The epochal victory of the capitalist west in the 20th century's defining political drama, culminating in the spectacular collapse of the USSR in 1992, precipitated the establishment of a truly global regime of capital accumulation that approximated the imaginaries proffered by Marx and Engels in the *Communist Manifesto* to a greater extent than at any other time since they penned their famous political call to arms some 150 years prior.

Within a few years of what establishment pundits incredibly termed 'The End of History', virtually all of the world's territorially bounded nation-states had acceded to the emergent international system, the political-economic order which would become known as neoliberal globalisation.[2] The fetters imposed on capital through the Cold War by organised labour and welfarism in the capitalist west, Third World nationalism in former European colonies, and actually existing socialism in the Soviet bloc were spectacularly and rapidly swept away by a combination of US-led 'humanitarian' military expeditions, coloured 'revolutions', offshoring and outsourcing, regional free trade agreements, and structural adjustment policies championed by the international financial institutions (IFIs).

Capital's liberation marked the crystallisation of a 'network society', in which ostensibly ubiquitous digital technology structured new modes of human life.[3] Within a generation, what became known as the Information and Communications Technology (ICT) revolution had engendered entirely new experiences of time, space and selfhood alongside, accompanied by notions that all humankind shared membership of the global 'village'.

Dizzying shifts in the global political economy were both the cause and consequence of an ideological offensive to reinscribe modernity at large. A history indelibly shaped by epic challenges to capitalism, colonialism and patriarchal social institutions across the globe was fantastically reduced to the ostensibly conjoined twins of 'democratic' liberalism and the 'free' market.[4] A universal human 'rationality' to match the prophecies of early modern Europe's bourgeois idealists was thus finally realised. Henceforth, *homo politicus* was to be the mirror of *homo economicus*, the 'invisible' hand of the self-correcting market and the rational subject of history flourishing together in a seamless march to neoliberal utopia.[5] For the first time, a hegemonic *politics* to match the universal logic of capital appeared uncontested on a world scale.

The universal claims of bourgeois 'civilisation' have a long genealogy in the non-western world. For more than 400 years, European colonisers across the globe ruled over territories inhabited by 'backward' peoples under the guise of improving and ultimately elevating them to the plane of cultural, economic and political modernity. The end of the Cold War sealed the long maturation of the hitherto primitive colonial subject into a 'free' individual engaging as the purported equal of former master and peer slave alike, in a truly global marketplace. Thirty years later, sloganeering about free markets and individuals alike rings hollow. The historic peripheries of the capitalist world-system are beset by more repression, violence, exploitation and dispossession than ever before.

In this book I elucidate the social-structural underpinnings of 'the political' in Pakistan at the current conjuncture, while making a modest addition to political theory in postcolonial South Asia and Sub Saharan Africa more generally. Capital's crisis-ridden march to a universal throne reveals the theoretical and practical terrain upon which revolutionary political action must be devised and enacted in times to come. A grounded theory of politics for the regions home to most of the world's population – formerly colonised South Asia and Sub-Saharan Africa – is necessary for the promise of universal emancipation to be realised. As Ranabir Sammadar suggests, '[t]he postcolonial condition makes Marx once again relevant'.[6]

If the idealised subject of capitalist modernity during the period of its consolidation in Europe was the bourgeoisie, then today this critical subject position in the non-western world is occupied by the so-called 'new middle class', depicted both as the motor of economic liberalisation and its primary beneficiary. This 'middle-class' subject has acquired an almost mythical status in South Asia and Sub-Saharan Africa, not to mention China, despite the depredations that neoliberalism has wrought. In short, a hegemonic middle-class ideology shapes politics and popular culture in much of the world. The hegemonic order thrives on the acute fallouts generated by the 'madness of economic reason' in postcolonial conditions, including but not limited to imperialist war, mass dispossession of 'surplus populations' and ecological degeneration.[7]

The spread of the novel coronavirus from China across the world in December 2019 briefly forced a reckoning with the brutalising realities of the global regime of capital accumulation, but the intellectual and political mainstream quickly moved on from nascent critique of the crisis-ridden system's urgent discontents. The pandemic has brought to light many glaring facts about the historically imperialised zones of the capitalist world-system, including deepening class conflict, rapacious pillage of natural resources, and majoritarian violence against oppressed castes, genders, ethnic nations and religious communities. Yet, an ideology of *middle-class aspiration* remains hegemonic.

This despite the fact that pandemic-induced shocks to the global accumulation regime forced many of those often clumsily described as 'middle class' back down into virtual pauperism overnight. Insofar as non-western 'emerging markets' have been the motor force of neoliberal globalisation, the pandemic illustrated that even slight disruption of capital and labour flows throughout the world dramatically impact the very existence of the so-called 'global middle class'.[8]

Consider India: an estimated 230 *million* people fell into poverty in the year after the pandemic began.[9] During intense and often brutally enforced lockdowns, countless Indian migrant workers were captured flooding out of metropolitan areas on foot, forced to walk thousands of kilometres to their ancestral villages. The circulation of such images online was a global event that hastened the rapid ascent of digitalised lifeworlds across the planet, a theme to which I will return throughout the course of the book. For the mythical 'global middle class' is at one and the same time produced by digitalisation and also its major protagonist.

In practice, digital spaces reflect profoundly uneven and exclusionary logics across different geographies and historical social formations of the world-system. At the height of the pandemic, these spaces nevertheless generated a visceral, collective experience of crisis far more pronounced than even a decade earlier when the political-economic fallouts triggered by the financial crash unfolded. The exponential growth of digital spaces in the months and years ahead – particularly in postcolonial countries like Pakistan – will grant them even more importance in the struggle for hegemony.

WHY MIDDLE-CLASS ASPIRATION?

The interlocking crises that afflict humanity and nature are multi-scalar, from the planetary down to the molecular level. Yet critical scholarship on the left remains skewed towards the Euro-American heartlands of capitalism. This book draws attention to the challenge of forging an alternative hegemonic conception in the historically imperialised zones of the world-system.

Rather than uncritically deploying the term 'new/global middle class' – a concept that I find misleading on several accounts – I will instead refer variously to specific social groups, e.g. 'state functionaries', 'urban consumers', 'contractors', and the like. It is only at this level of analysis that concepts hold weight to describe grounded realities of social class. I will reserve use of 'middle class' strictly to describe an *ideological* category, which is one of fundamental importance for understanding our world. I take the *aspiration* to be middle class in the non-western world as a central object of analysis.

Paradoxically, this aspiration has become even more widespread in non-western countries during an interregnum (2006–) that coincides with the implosion of middle-class hegemony in western societies. Though real wages in the western world have been stagnating and inequality on the march for decades, the political-economic upheavals triggered by the financial crisis of 2006–2008 rendered the contradictory political logics of neoliberalism's 'extreme centre' irreconcilable.[10] The illusions of 'progressive neoliberalism' – namely a politics of recognition consistent with 'middle-class' majoritarianism – were hence decisively shattered.[11]

The crisis of 'the political' that subsequently unfolded in western polities was embodied by self-proclaimed 'anti-establishment' politicians peddling racist, sexist and nationalist ideologies. The spectacle of Donald Trump and Boris Johnson being elected to power in the belly of the beast – alongside Le Pen, Salvini and many others that dramatically altered electoral calculus in the western political mainstream – was both cause and consequence of an ever more fetishistic and mediatised field of politics as financialisation and digitalisation proceeded apace.

> [C]ommercialised, entertainment-oriented media from the communicative content of a broader social environment, in which phenomena such as Donald Trump flourish. There are many causes of right-wing authoritarianism, and a fragmented, colonized, commercialized, commodified, accelerated public sphere is ... one of the influencing factors.[12]

A rich wave of critical theory has attempted to make sense of the far-right coming to power in Europe and North America, and elucidate emergent subjectivities in the wake of collapsing neoliberal hegemony.[13] More generally, theorising on matters as diverse as the ecological crisis and eco-socialism; automation and post-work society; 'digital' capitalism; and the commons/commoners have proliferated in the post-2008 period.[14]

Yet, for all its depth, most theorisations of contemporary capitalism and potentialities of its transcendence neither veer into the historically imperialised zones of the world-system nor raise the important question of the relationship between the floundering of neoliberal hegemony and the decline of the US Empire. The individual persons of Bolsonaro, Modi, Duterte, Imran Khan and others have garnered some attention, but, in general, the social-structural roots of contemporary authoritarianism in postcolonial contexts have generated very limited *theoretical* interest. Again, it is as if political and economic struggles in the postcolony have little purchase on the world.[15]

In this book I take a contrary view, arguing that we cannot understand the global crisis without centring attention on non-western, postcolonial regions, particularly Asia and Africa. In short, 'the so-called "global south" affords privileged insight into the workings of the world at large' for three interrelated reasons.[16]

First, the vast majority of the world's people live in postcolonial countries, with exponentially growing urban populations in South Asia and Sub-Saharan African especially prominent.[17] Second, South Asia and Sub-Saharan Africa are experiencing massive youth bulges; this segment of humanity is increasingly connected – both across physical space and via digital platforms

– to other regions and people within nation-state boundaries and beyond. This youthful demographic will greatly condition 'the political' in decades to come. Third, the worst fallouts of global warming/climate change, are, according to most scientific forecasts, expected to play out 'mainly in East and South Asia, between Pakistan and North Korea', where a significant majority of the world's youthful population resides.[18] The objective conditions facing this youthful mass in the next few decades can either precipitate more war/violence, inequality, authoritarianism and ecological destruction, or stimulate a new communist horizon.[19]

Asia was, of course, the critical frontier of neoliberalism in the aftermath of the Cold War, with Sub-Saharan Africa following close behind. India epitomised the neoliberal success story most of all, its celebrated middling strata confirming the 'miracle' of globalisation. Hundreds of millions of Indians, it has been widely and repeatedly asserted, were extricated from poverty to take their place in what has routinely been described as a 'global middle class'. Pakistan too boasts one of the biggest and fastest-growing middle strata in the world, estimated at over one-third of a total population of 230 million.[20]

A recent manuscript on the ubiquity of capitalism places upwardly mobile Indians, Chinese and other Asians at the centre of a global story:

> The uncontested dominion of the capitalist mode of production has its counterpart in the similarly uncontested ideological view that moneymaking not only is respectable but is the most important objective in people's lives, an incentive understood by people from all parts of the world. The fact that (to use Marxist terms) the infrastructure (the economic base) and superstructure (political and judicial institutions) are so well aligned in today's world not only helps global capitalism maintain its dominion but also makes people's objectives more compatible and their communication clearer and easier, since they all know what the other side is after. We live in a world where everybody follows the same rules and understands the same language of profit-making.[21]

Through the course of this book, I interrogate this claim, and particularly the 'middle-class' subject that is purportedly the embodiment of capitalist ideology; it is far from obvious that the middle class in much of the world is expanding seamlessly alongside a global 'language of profit-making', as the above account suggests.[22] Whether non-western middling strata are performing, and will continue to perform, historical roles as the primary protagonist of global capitalism also merits interrogation.

This book does not present an authoritative account of the non-western middle class *per se*. I neither undertake a quantitative assessment of the middle class nor detail the various professional occupations/livelihood strategies of those who fall into the middle-class bracket. Detailed and exhaustive recent studies have already accomplished much in this regard.[23] Also notable is a burgeoning literature on what can broadly be termed the cultural mores of the emergent middle classes.[24]

I engage with the above literature (among others) to argue against the hegemonic conception in Pakistan, which, to reiterate, is founded upon *middle-class aspiration*. In deploying the term *aspiration*, I operate from the premise that the 'middle class' exists in 'grey areas, ambiguously located in the social structure, inhabited by individuals whose trajectories are extremely scattered'.[25] To be sure, 'middle class' is an extremely slippery category – the narrative of hundreds of millions rising from humble backgrounds to 'middle-class' status is powerful precisely because of its haziness.

Neoliberalism's promise of depoliticised, 'free' markets and a fast-track to individual mobility is perpetually unhinged by the volatile political economy of neoliberalisation in practice.[26] In short, while acceding to the logics of the market and deeply ingrained patronage networks can facilitate mobility 'from below', the nexus of capital and state ultimately generates immiseration for many middle-class aspirants, as spectacularly demonstrated during the pandemic.

FEAR AND DESIRE

The depiction of a rising middle strata in non-western countries with sociological roots in the toiling classes, oppressed castes and peripheral ethnic-linguistic nations – not to mention prominent and vocal representation across genders and sexual preference – certainly contains a kernel of truth. The palpability of a 'better life' represents, in fact, the very foundations of the hegemonic order.

However, the choreographed production of hegemonic middle-class subjectivity in an increasingly digitalised field of politics also betrays the fact that, as Gramsci asserts, hegemony is always protected by the armour of coercion; the neoliberal developmental regime has systematically intensified processes of de-peasantisation, exploitation, dispossession and the creation of 'surplus populations', the (post) colonial state apparatus doubling down on established traditions of suppressing dissent alongside.

A now vast literature on contemporary practices of accumulation in non-metropolitan settings confirms what Rosa Luxemburg noted more than a century ago: '[T]he accumulation of capital, seen as an historical process, employs force as a permanent weapon, not only at its genesis, but further on down to the present day'.[27] This resort to force betrays the grandiose proclamations of endless prosperity that have defined the neoliberal age, thus exposing a volatile rather than stable hegemonic order.

To borrow from the evocative title of a book written on the contradictory totality of India's experience with neoliberal globalisation, the hegemonic appeal of being amongst 'the beautiful' is set against the spectre of becoming one of 'the damned'.[28] Even Branko Milanovic, who describes the current conjuncture as the 'uncontested dominion of the capitalist mode of production', acknowledges that the dominant ideology projects 'the belief that social mobility is more feasible than it really is'.[29]

In recent years, categories like the 'precariat' have risen to prominence in western contexts. Hundreds of millions of working people in South Asia and Sub-Saharan Africa have suffered various forms of exploitation, and precarity more generally, since long before the neoliberal epoch. The coercive and exclusionary nature of capitalist markets in many postcolonial societies, not to mention war, dispossession, and other manifestations of structural violence, have always been, and remain, brutalising to no end.[30] Exceptional moments like the COVID-19 pandemic simply confirm the systemic logics that keep the majority of working people in South Asian and Sub-Saharan Africa, *middle-class aspirations* notwithstanding, on a knife-edge.

I conceptualise middle-class hegemony in terms of a dialectic of *fear* and *desire.** 'Middle-class' aspiration engenders the accumulation of wealth through savings, interest and the acquisition of property and rental income so as to partake in conspicuous consumption. The desire for elevated social status both at home and in the digitalised 'global village' is dialectically conjoined to an 'other' that threatens both the middle-class subject and the political community to which the former pledges allegiance.

For the most part, this 'other' is physically proximate and therefore an imminent threat: the toiling classes; the disloyal ethnic/racial/religious community; women and other oppressed genders; political dissidents; and so on. There is always some 'other' that symbolises one's fears. The struggle 'from below' to secure some wealth and power entails not only competition with those of a similar aspiration, but rejection of those further down the status ladder, many of whose social identities render them intrinsically 'different' or 'other'.

The politics of fear is symbiotically connected to state nationalism. Ideological state apparatuses and the mass media continuously invoke the nebulous enemy that threatens from without. The domestic 'other' and the foreign enemy together constitute an unholy nexus that must be subjected at the very least to the watchful surveilling eye of the state, and, quite often, its strong-arm.

Indeed, as man-made disasters proliferate due to climate change/global warming and/or outbreaks of mass pandemics like COVID-19, fear and panic associated with an ostensibly Hobbesian state of nature will likely be instrumentalised by nation-states, or even global governing regimes, to generate consent for what some left theorists have termed 'Climate Leviathan'.[31] In the post 9/11 world, the so-called 'war on terror' has served explicitly authoritarian ends; in chapters to come I discuss how the politics of fear has been generated in Pakistan by the militarised state apparatus under the pretext of subduing the seemingly perennial threat of 'terrorism'.

PAKISTAN AS A LABORATORY OF NEOLIBERALISM

Forged in the crucible of colonialism, South Asian and African states have inherently authoritarian lineages. A militaristic con-

* I thank Hafeez Jamali for first getting me thinking about *fear* and *desire*.

fessional nationalism has been the dominant ideology of the state in Pakistan since soon after its creation. Pakistan's body-politic has also been characterised by an almost permanent state of legal exceptionalism, a recent manuscript even conceptualising it as a 'metacolonial state'.[32] Under the regime of neoliberal globalisation, Pakistan has not occupied pride of place in the corporate mainstream. In contrast to India and even Bangladesh, Pakistan's upwardly mobile segments have enjoyed little acclaim while its liberal democratic institutions have remained largely subservient to an omnipotent military establishment.

Yet both the intensification of repression due to the so-called 'war on terror' and fallouts of financialisation have been borne by working masses across all of South Asia. With the mythical 'global middle class' increasingly prone to supporting extremely reactionary political forces that raise the spectre of a tyranny of the majority, the trajectory of high-profile globalisers like India has, on the surface at least, converged with Pakistan, even if the accents in their respective brand of authoritarian politics remain distinct.

This book focuses on Pakistan largely for parochial reasons; my scholarly interests are supplemented by more than two decades of political and academic immersion in Pakistani society. Nevertheless, I suggest that Pakistan's particular case provides insights into 'the political' across the postcolonial world. The universalising tendencies of capital have intensified across almost all of South Asia and Sub Saharan Africa over the past three decades, with many similar effects.

Since the turn of the millennium, the intellectual and political mainstream – especially in western countries – has depicted Pakistan as an undependable and reluctant 'ally' of the 'free world' on account of a seemingly unending tryst with (a nebulously defined) terrorism. With the long arm of a praetorian army casting a shadow over the entire gamut of political and economic affairs, Pakistani society is routinely portrayed as a repository of 'extremist' currents.

Just like India, Bangladesh and 'emerging markets' in Africa, however, Pakistan was a neoliberal success story in the early 2000s motored by upwardly mobile urban consumers with access to cheap credit supplied by privatised commercial banks. Hot capital, most notably remittances from well-off diaspora communities in western countries fearing confiscation of assets after 9/11, flooded high-return sectors like real estate and the stock market. Meanwhile, multinational mining, agribusiness and construction companies were given free licence to intensify, and in many cases, initiate unprecedented schemes of expropriation while the IFIs pumped money into mega 'development' projects that dispossessed rural communities and hastened the collapse of already vulnerable ecosystems.[33]

Pakistan did not feature in neoliberal manuals as a mythical low-wage, feminised manufacturing haven as in the case of Bangladesh's garment industry, or a tech and pharmaceutical hub motored by youthful entrepreneurs like neighbouring India. However, by securing geopolitical rents, World Bank and IMF-trained technocrats managing Pakistan's economy in the shadow of dictatorship and war concocted their own version of a neoliberal economic haven.

The military government of General Pervez Musharraf presided over what was termed a 'TV revolution', as 24-hour news television transformed the mediascape and political communication more generally.[34] It was also in the early 2000s that the internet became accessible to a wide cross-section of the Pakistani population, heralding what was to become an almost ubiquitous smartphone 'culture', particularly amongst younger segments. This marked the birth of a youthful middle-class political subject, which, under the backdrop of the so-called 'war on terror', acted as a captive audience for a military junta that pronounced, for the umpteenth time, saving of the proverbial nation as its *raison d'etre*.

In sum, the Musharraf regime enacted a passive revolution (a la Gramsci), 'articulated around nodes of "development" and a praetorian nationalism, incorporating the newly emergent middle class into a reformulated historic bloc with the military retaining its central role'.[35] Consent generated within metropolitan centres like Karachi, Islamabad, and Lahore, the latter capital of the country's dominant and most developed region of central Punjab, was mirrored by brutalisation of historically oppressed ethnic peripheries. The inhabitants of the western border regions with Afghanistan, Balochistan and Khyber Pakhtunkhwa, bore the greatest brunt of imperialist war, armed insurgencies, and an attendant state of exception.

The neoliberal juggernaut established during the Musharraf regime has since diversified and expanded its tentacles across the length and breadth of the social formation. Real estate developers, bankers, media tycoons, stockbrokers, mining and building contractors, transporters, petty middle men of all kinds, and what on the Pakistani street are known as 'mafias', are the face of Pakistan's postcolonial capitalist order. They collaborate with state functionaries to accumulate power and capital while mediating the supply of basic goods and services. They are integrated both with global finance and the entrenched networks of political patronage that structure the Pakistani polity.

Politicians with lineages of landed influence dating to the colonial period, business magnates, diverse commercial segments, and religio-political forces comprise a ruling bloc in which a fragmented yet still powerful civilian state bureaucracy retains a mediating role vis a vis exploited classes, oppressed ethnic nations, castes, genders and religious groups.

At the apex of this political-economic structure sits the military institution and its vast network of retainers, which, in turn, is variously patronised by the US, Chinese, Saudi Arabian and other external powers. Having come into being as a 'garrison state' that broadly served the interests of western imperialism during the Cold War, Pakistan's external relations have always been overdetermined by rivalry with India.[36] This explains Beijing's close relations with Islamabad ever since the Sino-Indian border war of 1962. From the 1970s onwards, the Gulf kingdoms, Saudi Arabia most of all, also emerged as a major patron of Pakistan's ruling class, in part by the opening of their doors to millions of Pakistani immigrant workers.

This book does not interrogate regional and global geopolitics during the era of neoliberal globalisation *per se*. However, I wish to note here that ebbs and flows in relations between Pakistan's various external patrons and between these patrons and Pakistan's militarised state apparatus have, on the whole, contributed to the strengthening of the latter, the political weaponisation of religion, and consolidation of rentier macroeconomic logics. The Pakistani military has retained a monopoly over and remained the primary beneficiary of foreign policy, symbolised by both its ever-expanding corporate empire and steady securitisation of the polity.

The military had to endure a strategic retreat from its role as arbiter of political and economic power following the Musharraf regime's dramatic fall from grace in 2007–2008. Shifting geopolitical winds and the global economic meltdown after the financial crash generated anti-incumbency sentiment, triggering a mass movement led by the legal fraternity. Asset bubbles that had sustained high growth rates between 2002–2006 burst as foreign remittances dried up. A macroeconomic balance of payments crisis reached breaking point due to skyrocketing prices of crude through 2007, oil the single largest contributor to Pakistan's import bill.[37]

Through the neoliberal 'success' years, middle-class aspiration swelled alongside a fetish for commodities. Markets for air conditioners, washing machines, cellular phones, personal computers, cars and motorcycles proliferated as commercial banks issued plastic money and staggered payment options for fixed assets.[38] From 2006 onwards, however, widespread inflation, and, infamously, massive disruption in electricity provision to both household and commercial units, or what in Pakistan is known as 'loadshedding', precipitated a mini-revolt.[39]

The globalised middle-class subject which had come into being through the Musharraf years put in its lot with a street movement around the person of the Supreme Court Chief Justice, earlier removed by Musharraf in a soap-operaesque power game of palace intrigues inclusive of US imperial machinations. The movement was constituted largely by urban professionals, and, with major political parties in the rear, deployed a liberal idiom of 'rule of law' to challenge the dictatorial regime. It also marked the coming of age for the TV media, whose live broadcast protests precipitated the emergence of a new digital public. Nestled in the confines of living rooms and other private settings, this digital public lapped up a liberal language of rights absent a structural critique of the established order.[40]

Newly politicised, young and educated segments peopled a fledgling digital terrain, buttressing the 'rule of law' brigade led by the legal fraternity and TV media. This youthful segment was by all accounts a child of the neoliberal developmental regime over which the Musharraf junta presided. Perceiving themselves as rebels with a cause, they pronounced: [we] 'the children of "enlightened moderation" turn against you'.[41]

The purportedly 'law-abiding' young people who came of age during the Musharraf years foreshadowed a bigger youthful demographic, both at home and in the diaspora, that would claim to break with a long history of 'corrupt' political incumbents and usher in what was later called 'Naya Pakistan' (New Pakistan). Cricketer-turned-politician Imran Khan was in 2007 still a minor political player, but his Pakistan Tehrik-e-Insaf (PTI) party 'ultimately would develop a synergy with the students' movement and arguably were one of the main beneficiaries of the protest'.[42]

Imran Khan ascended to the prime ministership more than a decade later on the discursive back of the middle-class political subject forged under the Musharraf regime. Contemporary middle-class hegemony as embodied by the person of Imran Khan shares many similarities with that of the virtual cult-like status of Narendra Modi in neighbouring India; both leaders rely on a popular narrative rejecting the clientelism of entrenched political parties, the latter allegedly guilty of systematic corruption and poor records of delivering 'development'. The appeal of Modi and Khan, like so many of their contemporaries in both the west and postcolony, is greatly enhanced by digital networks.

As I have already noted, hegemony is crafted by fusing the desire for consumption and upward mobility to a fear of the proverbial 'other'. The latter can be located in the 'terrorist badlands' of Balochistan, Khyber Pakhtunkhwa, other ethnic peripheries like Sindh, Gilgit-Baltistan and the Siraiki belt of South Punjab, or take the form of racialised, gendered and caste-ised working populations in metropolitan centres. The criminalisation of the victims of war, indigenous communities expropriated in the name of 'development', women and girl-children, and the rural and urban toiling classes, underlines that capital still generates colonial logics of difference. The continuities between the neoliberal conjuncture and authoritarian moments that preceded it are, indeed, remarkably stark.

It is, in fact, essential to excavate historic hegemonies from the colonial period onwards so as to fully contextualise the current conjuncture. Notwithstanding periods of divergence, trajectories of politics in the historically imperialised zones of the capitalist world-system exhibit, with notable exceptions, significant similarity. I understand the contemporary wave of authoritarianism in many postcolonial contexts as both cause and consequence of massive demographic and technological change, and an attendant mass hegemonic subjectivity. Yet, new forms of hegemony also exhibit recurring characteristics. It is to these historical genealogies of 'the political' that I turn next.

THE CLASS THAT NEVER WAS

When British colonial administrator Thomas Babington Mccaulay proclaimed his infamous minute of education at Whitehall in 1835, he did more than outline the principles of colonial statecraft in India, and, for that matter, other parts of the British Empire. He was, in fact, outlining a pedagogical project for the *long duree* founded upon what Gramsci would call *direzione*, or 'moral and intellectual leadership'.

> We must at present do our best to form a class who may be interpreters between us and the millions whom we govern, a class of persons Indian in blood and colour, but English in tastes, in opinions, in morals and in intellect. To that class we may leave it to refine the vernacular dialects of the country, to enrich those dialects with terms of science borrowed from the western nomenclature, and to render them by degrees fit vehicles for conveying knowledge to the great mass of the population.[43]

The educated class of 'natives' certainly played the role that Mccaulay had envisioned, but the breakdown of foundational binaries in the colonial political economy – most notably between the educated and so-called 'dangerous' classes, the town and the countryside, and, ultimately, between the metropole and the colony – meant that the very 'men of letters' imagined as guarantors of colonisation would turn against it, becoming the vanguard of national liberation.[44] To adapt Ranajit Guha, 'the political' in the colonies was a dominance without *lasting* hegemony.

Yet, the national liberation project proffered by the 'native middle class' was beset with its own contradictions. At the height of global decolonisation, Fanon wrote:

> [A]n authentic national middle class ought to consider as its bounden duty to betray the calling fate has marked out for it, and to put itself to school with the people: in other words to put at the people's disposal the intellectual and technical capital that it has snatched when going through the colonial universities. But unhappily we shall see that very often the national middle class does not follow this heroic, positive, fruitful, and just path... [it] refuses to follow the path of revolution, [and] will fall into deplorable stagnation. It is unable to give free rein to its genius, which formerly it was wont to lament, though rather too glibly, was held in check by colonial domination.[45]

The notion that an 'authentic' national middle class would have realised the revolutionary potentialities of the national liberation struggle resonated with dominant intellectual histories of the time. Revisionist historiography has definitively debunked the narrative of the bourgeoisie – and/or middle class – as the vanguard of democracy, both in the annals of western modernity and Europe's colonies.[46] Indeed, Fanon's teacher Cesaire baulked at the notion that western 'civilisation – as it has been shaped by two centuries of bourgeois rule' could be given the name at all. For Cesaire, 'between colonization and civilisation there is an infinite distance', the former nothing more than a 'bridgehead in a campaign to civilise barbarism, from which there may emerge at any moment the negation of civilisation, pure and simple'.[47]

I would like to suggest that there never was an *authentic national middle class*. It didn't fail to achieve its historic duty because it never existed. In the event, the civilisational vision pursued by postcolonial nation-builders in the immediate post-independence period proved all too similar to that of the colonial masters that they replaced. The very icons of the freedom struggle that warned against the perils of 'neo-colonialism' relied on projects of modernisation 'from above'. In so doing, they inadvertently consolidated the rule of capital to the detriment of toiling classes, castes, ethnic-nations and genders, while continuing to instrumentalise nature and her resources.

Where national liberation movements boasted substantial revolutionary currents, the Soviet Union's umbrella and the politics of non-alignment offered the opportunity to loosen the grip of western imperialist powers on their former colonies, a point to which I will return later in the book. Ultimately, however, a popular hegemonic project to transcend capital and overhaul the authoritarian legal-institutional logics of colonial statecraft could not be realised. Instead, the postcolonial state's coercive and ideological apparatuses were often mobilised to undermine the popular bases of freedom movements. The terrain of politics was delimited in the name of the fledgling nation, the inheritors of state power tragically fulfilling Fanon's ominous prophecies. Or perhaps it is more accurate to posit that the real tragedy was the non-existence of an 'authentic national middle class' as an historical force.

THE FIRST MIDDLE-CLASS MOMENT

Scholarly attempts to theorise the postcolonial political settlement emphasised the leadership of the white-collar salaried class in a volatile coalition comprising an emergent industrial bourgeoisie, landed castes/'tribes' and other social forces with lineages of power from the colonial period. Bardhan's was the paradigmatic formulation for the Indian context.[48] Hamza Alavi offered another analytic for 'the political' in the immediate post-independence period – that of the overdeveloped state – but his formulation was neither dynamic nor attentive to the problematic of consent 'from below'.[49] In the African case, Mahmood Mamdani demonstrated that modern citizenship remained the preserve of the white settler. In contrast, the genius of the native was deemed unsuitable for modern citizenship, and s/he was hence declared a subject to be ruled according to 'tradition', mapped primarily in terms of tribal identity/affiliation.[50]

All of these formulations suggested a tenuous hegemony, based on a colonial dichotomy whereby the 'wretched of the earth' continued to inhabit a relatively unchanging social and cognitive world, while what Gramsci would call 'molecular transformation' was enforced by the proverbial *kala sahib* (black master)who had replaced the *gora sahib* (white master). Notwithstanding the image of nation-builders such as Nkrumah, Sukarno, Nasser and Nehru as anti-imperialist statesmen on the world stage, colonial cleavages continued to structure the domestic body-politic.

In India, the party of national liberation was both unable and unwilling to transcend its high caste, and peculiarly bourgeois (secular) moralism.[51] Pakistan's educated classes had no pretence about democracy or secularism at all. A little over a decade after the country came into being, a military dictatorship headed by General Ayub Khan was established in the name of what the superior judiciary called 'the doctrine of revolutionary legality'.[52]

Many decades later, the urbane and largely westernised 'old middle-class' looks back on the Ayub years with genuine nostalgia. In comparison to what later became a far more diverse middle strata, McCauley's educated interlocutors constituted but a 'small urban middle class' perceiving themselves to be the '"authentic" bearer of culture'. In a related vein, the Ayub Khan regime propagated a unitary 'moral vision' for the Pakistani nation, even though this vision was in fact 'class-specific'.[53]

The motif of 'corrupt' politicians counterposed to clean, efficient administrators – an idiom that harkened back to the Raj – was invoked as the primary reason for Ayub's coup. The coup-makers claimed to be arresting 'the ruthless struggle for power, corruption, the shameful exploitation of our simple, honest, patriotic and industrious masses, the lack of decorum and the prostitution of Islam for political ends'.[54] The language of 'corruption', as I will discuss in Chapter 2, has been revived in spectacular fashion in the contemporary iteration of 'middle-class' authoritarianism.

The extension of the colonial middle-class moment well into the post-independence period was certainly not just a discursive technology of rule. For the most part, the educated classes supported the unitary state apparatus in the sustenance of combined and uneven developmental logics. When what were deemed 'backward' areas like Balochistan made 'demands for provincial status and autonomy, share in power and due share in civil and military bureaucracy, they were denied it on the basis of the supposed lack of "enough educated personnel" or the lack of "capacity" to administer the province'.[55]

Inhabiting what they considered 'modern', bourgeois lifeworlds did not deter state managers from reinforcing classed, racialised, caste-ised, gendered and other logics of 'traditional' power inherited from colonial rule. The successor states of the British Raj appeared to embark on very different political trajectories, but in the final analysis even the enshrining of formal 'democratic' institutions did not undermine the authoritarian bases of the everyday state, India's 'political economy of development' closely resembling Pakistan's 'political economy of defence', both polities betraying hegemonic pretensions that scarcely transcended colonial antecedents.[56]

Soon enough, capital's inexorable logic of expansion would expose the narrow, brittle foundations of this hegemonic political settlement. By the late 1960s, the social formation governed by the colonial-era ruling bloc was jolted by class, caste, gender and other contradictions that shaped new political subjectivities and forms of mobilisation. The premise that only a privileged segment of society – many amongst the educated 'middle classes' were actually the progeny of landed notables – could participate in the formal public sphere, and articulate political ideas therein, was certainly contested by toiling classes, oppressed ethnic nations, castes, genders and religious groups throughout the colonial encounter, as revisionist historiography like early subaltern studies scholarship demonstrated so vividly four decades ago. Yet, even the pretence of a 'public' and 'political' delineated by class and other markers of colonial-era privilege was decisively shattered by the social and political movements of the late 1960s and 1970s.

Those uprisings were animated by transformative imaginaries of class/caste revolution, a world free of imperialism, and, in western societies, of liberation from patriarchal bondage and sexual repression. With left-progressives and youth in the lead, Pakistan's popular movement forced General Ayub Khan to abdicate in 1969. Progressive parties swept the country's first election the following year. But counter-revolution quickly followed, triggered by the military establishment's action in East Pakistan. After the latter seceded to form Bangladesh in December 1971, a truncated Pakistan remained in the grip of revolutionary fervour. By the middle of the decade, however, dreams of the revolutionary transformation of state and society had turned sour.

THE SEARCH FOR A REVOLUTIONARY SUBJECT

Fanon poignantly articulated the contradictory fact of anticolonial and revolutionary movements being led by the same men of letters originally envisioned as the vanguards of colonial paternalism. He warned accordingly of the native intellectual's fallibility even while extending the latter's revolutionary subjectivity to its contingent limits. The colonised 'middle-class' political subject was not *destined* to play a certain historical role – just as the working class of 20th-century revolutionary yore did not.[57] The heyday of revolutionary internationalism, which persisted until the 1970s, was distinctive precisely because of the 'vortex of unprecedented intellectual, social, and political ferment … This was a world in which anything, and everything, seemed possible'.[58]

No matter what the structural determinants – imposed by capital and state, expressed within the confines of the formal public sphere – the utter contingency of politics reared its head, time and again. For Fanon, the native intellectual could transcend his Manichean origins through a combination of struggle within the self and for the proverbial nation more broadly. A revolutionary dialectics could herald 'national consciousness … accompanied by the discovery and encouragement of universalising values'.[59]

Pakistan's nascent revolutionary left – or, more specifically, its leadership – was constituted largely of individuals from the native gentry exposed to insurrectionary ideologies, often as students in the mother country. Communist leaders criminalised for challenging state and class power in Pakistan's early years in fact had remarkably close – sometimes even familial – ties to high-ranking state personnel in both of the successor states to the British Raj.[60]

The Communist Party of Pakistan (CPP) remained at the frontline of resistance to unitary state nationalism, class domination and reactionary ideologies even after its banning in 1954 and Pakistan's accession to US-sponsored Cold War security pacts in Asia. Yet, the left's leadership – and the movements of resistance of which the CPP was at the forefront – was always pushing beyond its weight with respect to organising the proverbial workers and peasants through and for whom revolution was to be made. Leftist strongholds were to be found in literary circles, print journalism and amongst college and university-going students. The left's substantial influence within the intelligentsia explains the force with which the coercive state apparatus clamped down upon leaders of the CPP, and its most effective front, the Progressive Writer's Association.[61]

For the first few years after formal independence, the left struggled to transcend its own narrow basis within the educated classes. By the late 1950s, transformation of the colonial political economy threw up a nascent trade union movement within the small industrial working class alongside a restive peasantry mobilising against landed and other rural influentials.

The revolutionary political subject of classical Marxist as well as closer-to-home Maoist texts hence appeared to be taking physical form, the left intelligentsia playing out its historical role as the bearer of revolutionary consciousness. The latter, however, did not necessarily break with the hegemonic logic of modernisation – and thereby of capital – propagated both by the Pakistani state and its western imperialist backers. The CPP's revolutionary horizon was a mechanical progressivism; its first secretary-general Sajjad Zaheer describing, in 1953, 'the contemporary period as that of industrialisation, capitalism and imperialism. Logically in this teleological schema the next stage would be communism (via socialism)'.[62]

This vision was symptomatic of its age. The revolutionary left across the world was committed to some or the other variant of Lenin's famous equation of communism to 'soviet power plus electrification of the whole country'.[63] Yet in Pakistan's case, not unlike other postcolonial contexts, this was oddly out of sync with social relations and productive forces. The industrial proletariat, understood in classical Marxist canon as 'free' wage labour, constituted only a fraction of the working population at large. Even when at its most organised, in the early 1970s, it was mobilised as often by appeals to ethnic solidarity as a universal proletarian identity.[64]

Burgeoning struggles in the countryside were easier to conceptualise in tandem with the actual class dynamics and demographics of the social formation. Through the 1960s and 1970s, significant pockets of the small and landless peasantry were mobilised for land reform by different left groups. Yet, what Lenin might have termed left-wing infantile disorder resulted in many strategic blunders, including a propensity to seek alliances within the bureaucratic state apparatus, which proved fatal for the country's largest peasant movement in the Hashtanagar area of Pashtun-majority Khyber Pakhtunkhwa.[65]

More generally, intense state repression, Pakistan's highly vexed 'national question', and an 'underground' existence dominated by prosaic and highly factional debates hindered the realisation of a national-popular will to challenge propertied classes, the militarised postcolonial state and imperialist powers.[66] Under the ostensibly centre-left Pakistan People's Party regime (1972–1977), the radical left faced intense state repression, leading to its virtual liquidation.[67]

THE INTERMEDIATE CLASSES

While mass politics in the non-western world of the 1960s and 1970s featured left-wing trade unionism, mobilisation of the small/landless peasantry, and student activism, as significant, though less emphasised, was the political coming of age of what, following the seminal work of Michael Kalecki, has been called the 'intermediate classes'.[68] I have discussed at length elsewhere how traders, merchants, small manufacturers, transporters, smallholding farmers and petty commodity producers of many other stripes, spread out across small towns and in metropolitan centres, one foot in their ancestral villages, another in their new, migrant abodes, erupted onto Pakistan's political-economic stage in the aftermath of the Green Revolution, mobilising religion, caste, and many more identities to demand a share of a previously insular political settlement.[69]

In the subcontinent and many other parts of the postcolonial world, the emergence of the intermediate classes signalled an end to the hitherto unchallenged political monopoly of the colonial educated classes and landed aristocrats. The intermediate classes were the 'nouveau-riche' of their time, unschooled in bourgeois ethics yet craving political power commensurate with their growing economic clout. A product of organic upward mobility 'from below', the intermediate classes were skilled in the logics of patronage politics, ruthless in their accumulation of capital, and with no commitment *per se* to either liberal or democratic mores.

The second middle-class moment (1977–1999), then, was both similar and different from that which preceded it. The logics of accumulating capital and power that inhered under conditions of what mainstream scholarship collapses under the term 'informality' were forged and defended through political ideologies and practices that undermined the universal claims of previously unchallenged national liberation movements. If hegemonic political forms in the three decades after WWII were expressed along the broad spectrum of grand ideologies like socialism – including 'Islamic', pan-African and Ba'athist variants – secularism, and state-led developmentalism, these now gave way to the economics of liberalisation and many different articulations of identity politics. Meanwhile, the emancipatory political subject with universal, largely male, pretensions – the industrial proletariat, anticolonial freedom fighter, the peasant guerrilla – was displaced by many particular political subjects.

An obituary of Nehruvian hegemony, which reached its nadir under Indira Gandhi's emergency, reads:

> Those who would see present difficulties as 'failures' of Indian capitalism would find it difficult to explain it. It is the 'successes' of Indian capitalism that have caused them. So if it becomes more successful in the ways it has pursued over the last twenty years, these problems would not go away, but perhaps intensify. The tragic thing is that the crisis of ruling-class politics plunges not only the ruling bloc into serious disorder but the whole country, the festival of which we are celebrating. Exhaustion of the politics of the ruling bloc does not automatically prefigure a radical alternative.[70]

In fact, the exhaustion of the earlier ruling bloc precipitated the establishment of another. As the logic of capital deepened in the social formation, transforming city and countryside, centres and peripheries, the emergent intermediate classes jostled with the colonial-era propertied classes for political, economic and cultural power. This struggle focused on control of state institutions, alongside what Gramsci would call the trenches of civil society, including new and old political parties alike.

With the initiation of what were euphemistically called economic 'reforms' by most Third World governments in the late 1980s, yet another iteration of middle-class ideology was christened. The establishment of the regime of neoliberal globalisation after the collapse of the Soviet bloc in the 1990s would eventually lend hegemonic status to what is the third – and contemporary – middle-class moment in postcolonial South Asia and Sub-Saharan Africa.

THEORISING POLITICAL SUBJECTS

The rupture in a previously insular 'public' and an attendant expansion of political forms and practices led, as in India following the Mandal Commission of 1989, to a definitive shift in

> the distribution of power, functioning of state institutions and economic relations in the countryside. The explicit appeal to caste identities by the regional parties that emerged in the 1990s sought to inspire a popular political mobilisation that potentially included the vast majority of the population in an attempt to subvert a long history of upper-caste hegemony.

That 'democracy', broadly conceived, has opened up opportunities for some working people, Dalits, women, and others from India's vast population of oppressed and exploited communities, certainly represents 'much more than a "politics of identity" for its own sake'.[71] Similar processes of 'democratisation' – insofar as this refers to historically excluded subalterns exercising distinct forms of agency in the everyday political realm – have taken place in other parts of the non-western world.

Theorisations of politics have followed this expansion of the public sphere and emergence of political forms that both liberalism and revolutionary Marxism could not previously decipher – a 'politics of the governed'; 'democracy against development'; even 'life as politics'.[72] These various attempts at crafting a theory of politics centering the variegated political subjects emerging in everyday social life are certainly not reducible to theorisations of 'left populism' in western metropolitan contexts, but a shared imperative can be detected – to potentiate a radical democratic politics not based on some prefigured idea of *one* emancipatory subject but hegemonised through agonisms in the actually existing polity.[73]

Other theorisations of 'the political' which also seek to transcend the *cul-de-sac* of Eurocentric interpretative frames make for less optimistic reading, portending the majoritarianism that has reared its head in the third – and contemporary – middle-class moment. Bayart's 'politics of the belly' offers a rich theorisation of politics in Sub-Saharan Africa, emphasising the ravages of dependency on a regional/global scale, entrenched practices of patronage in society, and the inescapably authoritarian essence of (post)colonial state institutions. Increasingly ruthless competition for wealth and political power certainly reflects an ever-expanding 'public', but class, ethnicity, 'tribal', caste, gender and other forms of historic privilege continue to structure political life.[74]

The political agency of the intermediate strata in Pakistan, as I have already suggested, corroborates the narrative frame of 'the politics of the belly'. 'Democratisation' has largely been associated with a widening circle of patronage. After a chastening eleven-year long military dictatorship ended in 1988, the restoration of formal bourgeois-democratic institutions was accompanied by the growing influence of the religious right and ethnic supremacist organisations, generating new anxieties.[75]

The work of scholars such as Oskar Verkaaik, Humeria Iqtidar and Sadaf Ahmad nevertheless challenges the assumption that otherwise 'illiberal' manifestations of right-wing politics reflect an incomplete modernity and 'underdeveloped' political consciousness. In some of these sophisticated readings, the Muslim woman – veiled, associated with Islamist causes of various hues – expresses political potentialities otherwise denied her by dominant scholarly and journalistic tropes.[76]

In sum, an expanded 'public' and myriad forms of political agency that have developed forthwith are both cause and consequence of the 'democratisation' of state and society, broadly conceived. This in turn has provided fertile ground for novel theorisations of politics beyond entrenched Eurocentric notions of the rational, liberal subject as the building block of democratic politics.

In my reading, however, the radical potentialities of both such theories and practices of politics are largely constrained by an exploitative and oppressive structural universe that remains inescapably colonial, capitalist and patriarchal. To be sure, the accent in most of the theorisations to which I have referred here is on the *possibility* of social mobility and recognition, through what is best described as acquiescence to the established rules of the game. Whether the emergent political subject chooses to put in her/his lot with some form of collective action, and/or elects more individuated strategies of navigating social and political worlds, caste-based, gendered, racialised, and classed structures are largely reinforced.

The real political subjects that took shape a generation removed from the revolutionary upsurges of the 1960s and 1970s may have demolished the hegemonic foundations of the first middle-class moment, but broadly acceded to emergent hegemonic imaginaries and forms of the second middle-class moment. At the dawn of the new millennium, Zaidi remarked that 'urban middle classes … are largely interested in fulfilling their narrow economistic goals and interests, as well as those related to the acquisition of power through whatever means possible'.[77] A third, authoritarian middle-class moment had well and truly been birthed.

A UNIVERSAL THEORY AND PRACTICE OF POLITICS?

With the steady displacement of revolutionary imaginaries by more pragmatic and multifarious political subjects 'from below', otherwise sophisticated and incisive theorisations of 'the political' in the non-western world have, in recent times, rarely engaged with the problematic of anti-systemic, 'universalist' politics.

It would be remiss to neglect mention of the wider context within which theorisations of postcolonial politics has evolved over the past few decades. Some years have now passed since a wide spectrum of scholarship somewhat lazily clumped into the epithet 'postcolonial studies' reached its zenith in the western academy. I do not seek to reopen a debate here, which has, for the most part, run its course.[78] What I want to flag is that the latter trajectory of postcolonial studies was, in the tradition of the post-modern turn more generally, characterised by a distrust, and effective rejection, of universalist politics, both in theory and practice.

The polemical debates that took place over many years often revolved around a somewhat esoteric 'materialism', and, further, the 'metanarrative' of Marxism. The latter was of course a major force in national liberation struggles across Asia, Africa and Latin America in the 20th century. It makes sense, then, that Marxian theories and related political forms have been the subject of significant and heated debate within both political and intellectual circles, especially after the revolutionary upsurges through the 1970s gave way to a period of intense reaction in the 1980s.

I wish only to note here that the ascendance of postcolonial studies coincided with both a relative decline in class analysis and revolutionary politics more generally.[79] It was thus within not 'a uniform intellectual or political lineage but a certain milieu' that one can reasonably place many theorisations of postcolonial politics, most notably in India, as neoliberal hegemony took root on a world scale at the turn of the millennium.[80]

There was certainly good reason to be sceptical of an epistemic paradigm that, according to its critics, assumed that the proverbial 'rest' would follow the trajectory of the 'west'. But while economic, cultural and political forms in imperialised zones of the world-system have always been distinct, neoliberal globalisation marked a qualitatively new phase in the historical evolution of postcolonial societies. The dramatic undoing of the fetters on capital that had persisted since formal independence generated *universally* hegemonic forms and political subjectivities that, in my reading, have yet to be fully comprehended.

The discursive formation that has developed in, *and about*, postcolonial contexts during the 30 years of neoliberal globalisation certainly confirms the universalising tendency of capital, including its most fetishised representation, the commodity.

> The world in its commodity form is imagined and ordered along a scale of temporality that mimics the earlier discourse of development. If developed, developing, and underdeveloped were the stages of modernity that defined the mid-twentieth-century decolonized world, the categories of

> developed, emerging, frontier, and preemerging mimic those, albeit in the twenty-first-century framework of markets … The idea of the third world has not expired; it has simply expanded in new locations … The postcolony-turned-emerging frontier is neither lagging behind nor playing catch-up; it foreshadows the ways in which the global political economy is being reshaped.[81]

As I noted at the outset, virtually all of the world's nation-states acceded to the global neoliberal regime following the end of the Cold War. For South Asian, Sub-Saharan African as well as relatively more 'developed' economies in East Asia and Latin America, this translated into adoption of the homogenising policy matrix that became known as the 'Washington Consensus'.[82] Removal of barriers for imports and restrictions on foreign investments; liberalisation of financial markets; rapacious 'enclosure of the commons'; privatisation of state-owned enterprises; reduction in social welfare spending; and wage cuts and devaluation of local currencies were some of the major precepts of so-called structural adjustment programmes championed by the International Monetary Fund and other IFIs. These programmes represented the primary modality through which postcolonial societies were initially incorporated into the regime of neoliberal globalisation.

I mention this well-known recent history to foreground once again the imperative of theorising postcolonial politics in dialectical relation with the global political economy. The regime of neoliberal globalisation has effectively reduced the entire practice of 'democracy' to a technocratic management exercise in which domestic ruling blocs vie to convince foreign investors that their country's 'emerging market' is the most attractive. Mainstream politics then revolves around securing a share of the returns from increasingly financialised practices of accumulation, while reinforcing local patronage networks.[83]

Meanwhile, politics 'from below', as discussed above, is a largely pragmatic exercise of navigating the everyday state and market. For those who can either objectively be considered, or perceive themselves to be, 'middle-class investor-citizens', this navigation can be idealised as opportunity to 'divert their individual capital to the domestic markets' and 'profit from the growing economy and multiply their personal capital'.[84]

For historically oppressed segments, and the toiling classes more generally, navigating state and market can hardly be romanticised. But as some of the theoretical arguments referenced earlier suggest, conscious strategies and alignments nevertheless debunk notions of the proverbial 'poor' as simply victims of an indomitable structure of power.

SANYAL AND 'SURPLUS POPULATIONS'

Kalyan Sanyal's ambitious attempt to explicate everyday political forms in India under the structural backdrop of 'primitive accumulation, governmentality and postcolonial capitalism' represents an important advance from the previous generation of postcolonial theory, a sophisticated attempt to delineate agency 'from below' in conversation with multiple higher analytical scales in the context of neoliberal globalisation.[85]

Sanyal's argument foregrounds what Marx called 'primitive' or 'primary' accumulation, offering the corrective that the latter is constitutive of capitalism in postcolonial conditions rather than reflective, as Marxist canon has often insisted, of a social formation still in transition to the fully developed capital–wage labour dialectical form. Capital's relentless tendency to expropriate primary producers and natural economies plays out contemporaneously in India – Sanyal's primary case study – as well as other postcolonial contexts.

Sanyal then layers this premise with another theoretical claim, namely that instead of the capital–wage labour relation, postcolonial capitalism features a distinct dialectic; as capital expands across the social formation, most of the population separated from the land – and, for that matter, other means of production like forest and water – is forced to turn to self-employment to make ends meet:

> Bereft of any direct access to means of labour, the dispossessed are left only with labour power, but their exclusion from the space of commodity production does not allow them to turn their labour power into a commodity. They are condemned

> to the world of the excluded, the redundant, the dispensable, having nothing to lose, not even the chains of wage-slavery.[86]

The empirical facts bear Sanyal out – approximately 40% of the labour force in Pakistan, for instance, is self-employed. But the theoretical formulation that follows with regards to the political subjectivity of these 'surplus populations' leaves, in my opinion, much to be desired.

Sanyal suggests that the self-employed mass occupies a separate economic sphere from the dominant one shaped in its image by capital. In the 'need economy', economic activities are guided not by the logic of capital but only by the imperative of subsistence. He then links this household-level analytic to the macro-political economy, noting how welfare interventions by government so as to secure legitimacy buttress the 'need economy', thereby ameliorating, if not reversing, the effects of primitive accumulation.

Sanyal claims that this relatively stable coexistence – mutual dependence, even – of separate spheres of economic activity is what accords hegemony to the postcolonial capitalist regime. 'Development' is a hegemonic idea that allows both for the dispossession of primary producers to facilitate capital *alongside* the provision of subsistence to the dispossessed. This dialectical process ensures that 'surplus populations' do not become the gravediggers of capitalism that Marx understood the 'reserve army of labour' would become.[87]

While I certainly concur with Sanyal about the pretensions of the neoliberal developmental regime, I have already established that the contemporary hegemonic order in postcolonial societies is highly volatile. In my understanding, many of those dispossessed to serve the interests of capital and state do *not* necessarily acquire access to means of labour to meet their needs.

Chatterjee argues to the contrary:

> [W]hile there is a dominant discourse about the importance of growth, which in recent times has come to mean almost exclusively capitalist growth, it is, at the same time, considered unacceptable that those who are dispossessed of their means of labour because of the primitive accumulation of capital should have no means of subsistence.[88]

Perhaps it is 'considered unacceptable that those who are dispossessed ... should have no means of subsistence' in instances where the dispossessed do not represent a threat to 'middle-class' civility. But as I will show through the course of this book, recurring crises, in new and old peripheries alike, regularly throws up what Chatterjee deems 'unacceptable' depredations.

Sanyal, I think, is correct to identify the unique features of postcolonial capitalism, but errs in denying capital's universalising pretensions. It is entirely plausible to argue that capital's march is relentless, forever transforming all that it encounters in its path, and that these encounters generate distinct forms – economic, political, cultural – under postcolonial conditions. The large numbers of dispossessed people who rely on self-employment to meet subsistence needs do so by engaging with capitalist markets. The circulation of commodities – from which virtually no human on the planet is disconnected – is as constitutive of the logic of capital as any process of (re)production.[89]

Indeed, contemporary hegemony in the postcolonial world is founded precisely on the notion, however illusory, that the toiling majority, including the self-employed, can in fact secure upward mobility through strategic insertion into circuits of capital. '[T]he extraordinary *aam aadmi* (ordinary man), who privileges personal gain as a form of nation building ... has defined the kind of self-centred, middle-class politics that has gained strength in the Indian polity'.[90]

Sanyal's analytic is powerful insofar as it suggests that the *aam aadmi* can and does negotiate with the welfarist institutions of government so as to secure subsistence. Further, the *aam aadmi* with the requisite savvy can him/herself become an 'investor-citizen' to profit in the proverbial marketplace. But hegemony is fragile because, more often than not, the *aam aadmi* does *not* become the investor-citizen, instead standing on the precipice of deprivation, subjected to capital's ruthless logic of accumulation and/or an authoritarian postcolonial state apparatus.

In this sense, 'developmental' institutions at best seek to incorporate surplus populations into the sphere of circulation. Sanyal's service to radical scholarship – and, by extension, left politics – is to force us to move beyond notions of an 'incomplete' capitalism that have long dogged Marxist theorisations of the postcolony.

But displacing the capital–wage labour dialectic as a hegemonic category does not automatically accord 'development' an unchallengeable hegemony in the manner that Sanyal contends.[91]

Put differently, 'the task is not to provincialise Europe or the world of metropolitan capital, but to universalise the postcolonial predicament'.[92] As more and more working people are subjected to the structural and physical violence of capital's universalising logic, the imperative of rehabilitating a universal–particular dialectic that can inform both theory and practice of politics becomes more urgent. It is only in and through such a dialectical understanding that progressives can transcend unhelpful debates that oppose 'identity' to class/capital.

THE ARGUMENT: A ROAD MAP

It will be useful to summarise my central claims here. To grasp the global crisis of capitalism and liberal politics, we must accord centrality to postcolonial capitalist societies. Doing so requires interrogating *middle-class aspiration* as the ideological prop of contemporary hegemony in these societies. Postcolonial capitalism *strives* for hegemony via an idealised middle-class subjectivity, but it is crisis-ridden, in similar yet different ways to social formations in the western heartlands of the capitalist world-system. Postcolonial capitalism seeks to create 'middle-class' consumers so as to ensure that profits are realised in the sphere of circulation, yet at the same time brutalises many of these potential consumers both overtly and through the economic coercion of markets that are laden with ethnic, caste, gender, religious and other forms of historical privilege.

To theorise politics 'from below', then, is to be attentive to two parallel realities. First, we must acknowledge the relatively banal everyday navigation of state and market, or what I have previously called the 'politics of common sense'. Second, we must be cognizant of the violent upheavals – wars, ecological breakdowns and profit-motivated dispossessions – that have increased manifold under the regime of neoliberal globalisation. Indeed, such upheavals have become more dramatic since the turn of the century, starting with the so-called 'war on terror' (2001–), then the political-economic crisis triggered by the financial crash (2006–2008), and most recently the novel coronavirus (2019–).

The dystopian prospect of political life being reduced to increasingly authoritarian management of docile and alienated middle-class subjects impels a reengagement with the potentialities of a universalist politics, of a world beyond the commodity form and self-enclosed identities. The intensifying challenge of climate change in any case demands a reckoning with our collective future. Dipesh Chakrabarty puts it thus: '[C]limate change poses for us a question of a human collectivity, and us pointing to a figure of the universal that escapes our capacity to experience the world. It is more like a universal that arises from a shared sense of a catastrophe'.[93]

Chakrabarty is, of course, a highly celebrated postcolonial theorist, and it is significant that he is now calling for humankind to strive for a 'planetary' consciousness to cope with the challenges to both our species and all other forms of life. In any case, a universalist politics for the present and the future cannot be confined to consideration of the mores, subjectivities, and wider structuring forces in the traditional heartlands of the capitalist world-system.

A shift in the balance of power within the capitalist world-system has already taken place under the regime of neoliberal globalisation, China asserting itself with increasing clarity as a superpower with global ambitions. In the next chapter, I analyse China's 'developmental' footprint in Pakistan through the China–Pakistan Economic Corridor (CPEC), the flagship project of the Belt and Road Initiative (BRI).

Constraints of space mean that I do not engage in this book with the prospect of China's emergent leadership in the world-system *per se*. However, China's political-economic trajectory during the regime of neoliberal globalisation shapes many of the concerns of this book. For the past three decades, upward mobility for a significant segment of the Chinese population has been coeval with growing inequality, ecological degradation and surveillance. Contending with an authoritarian and increasingly digitalised social order hegemonised around the consent of a pliant middle-class subject is thus a challenge facing progressives in many different historical social formations across the globe.

In the wake of COVID-19, it is ever more urgent to contemplate political theory and practice within universal frames, and, further, to accord primary to the empirical realities of the historically imperialised zones of the world-system. To reiterate: it is in South Asia and SSA that a majority of the world's people live, most of them young and increasingly connected via digital media. This youthful majority can, as I see it, remain spellbound to a dialectic of fear and desire, or chart new hegemonic forms that signal an end to the brutalisation of the proverbial 'other', and their own selves.

Capital's relentless march in postcolonial societies continues to generate 'difference' on the basis of caste, ethnicity, gender and religion. By acknowledging and at the same time challenging this foundational logic of postcolonial capitalism – in both its historical and contemporary guises – it is possible, I submit, to craft a theory of emancipatory politics for our time.

The historic trajectory of capital in the postcolony has, of course, been intimately tied to the logic of colonial statecraft. It is, therefore, to the dialectic of state and capital that I turn first. In Chapter 1, I adapt Gramsci's concept of the 'Integral State' to elucidate Pakistan's prevailing structure of power in which a militarised state apparatus collaborates with domestic and foreign capital to pillage nature via an increasingly financialised accumulation regime. Large segments of society – both those harbouring middle-class aspirations as well as the subordinate classes more generally – are co-opted into matrices of economic and political power through networks of patronage.

Systematic dispossession of indigenous and other working-class communities to facilitate capital accumulation is both cause and consequence of increasingly monopolistic and commodified markets for basic needs like housing, water and food. Mafioso-like elements in trade, manufacturing, and land development rely on and extend profits to both the military establishment and functionaries of the civilian bureaucratic apparatus, so that the lines between crime and 'lawful' accumulation are blurred.[94] Through selected vignettes set across Pakistan's uneven developmental geographies, I demonstrate that the most acute and ultimately irreconcilable contradiction generated by this multi-scalar accumulation regime is an ecological one.

In Chapter 2, I turn specifically to the making of the middle-class subject, and the politics of *fear* and *desire*. Hegemonic political subjectivity has always been shaped by the nexus of state and capital, with the mass media playing an increasingly central role in postcolonial societies. I show how 'state of exceptions' are established – both historically and in the current conjuncture – to generate fear within captive urban populations. The paradigmatic case study of the chapter plays out under the backdrop of the so-called 'war on terror'. Indiscriminate military operations in the Baloch and Pashtun peripheries have, with few exceptions, been cheered on by metropolitan Pakistanis. Meanwhile, migrant workers displaced from their ancestral lands in past and present iterations of imperialist war, climate breakdown and de-peasantisation are subject to racial discrimination and criminalisation in urban centres under the guise of 'counter-terrorism'.

In Chapter 3, I analyse how hegemony – both dominant and embryonic popular forms – is crafted in an increasingly digitalised field of politics. The very idea of the 'public' has been transformed, with the digital space becoming the site of unprecedented politicisation of gender, class, ethnic and other historical social faultlines. I counterpose divisive and reactionary political forms and movements to progressive political and social struggles that owe at least some of their popular, potentially hegemonic appeal, to the digital space. In particular, I look at movements mobilised by young affectees of the 'war on terror' in ethnic peripheries challenging extant state and imperialist ideology, and burgeoning expressions of feminism in metropolitan centres that challenge increasingly fragile and reactionary patriarchal norms. It is in this digital space that a prolonged 'war of position' is set to play out, featuring mass surveillance, commodification, and atomisation on the one hand, and potential hegemonisation of universalist political ideas and practices on the other hand.

In Chapter 4, I sketch out the barebones of a theory of emancipatory politics by deploying the signifier of the 'classless subject'. This revolutionary imaginary acknowledges the real history of capital and its (re)production of difference and the particularisms of subject positions, yet still posits a universal subject of emancipation. To bring to life this 'classless subject' is to transcend the 'competition of oppressions' that play out in the digitalised echo chambers of progressive politics between variegated subjects resisting capital, ethnic-racial oppression and patriarchy. As pandemics, climate change, militarism and dispossession intensify alongside the banal everyday functioning of capitalist markets and state power, Rosa Luxemburg's age-old refrain of humanity being faced with a choice between socialism and barbarism will become even more poignant. This choice will be confronted, among others, by exactly that middle-class subject produced by but ultimately excluded from the contemporary hegemonic order.

Either way, the historically imperialised zones of the world-system will play a vital role in charting the future of 'the political' for humankind on the whole. As Samir Amin reminds us, 'the peoples of the peripheries of the system, which is polarising by nature, have a long experience of positive, progressive nationalism, which is anti-imperialist, and rejects the global order imposed by the centres, and therefore is potentially anti-capitalist'.[95]

1
The Integral State

> [T]he State is the entire complex of practical and theoretical activities with which the ruling class not only justifies and maintains its dominance, but manages to win the consent of those over whom it rules.
>
> Antonio Gramsci, SPN 244, Q15, §10

Contra to mainstream historiography, what became the modern bourgeois state in the western heartlands of the capitalist world-system was decidedly *un*democratic. Early modern state-making often resembled 'organised crime', militarised polities undergoing a gradual and conflict-ridden process of civilianisation.[1] The advent of 'democracy', then, owed itself as much to struggles *against* the bourgeoisie as it did to the latter's wilful leadership.

It was to make sense of the contradictory dynamics and repercussions of the relatively novel phenomenon of mass representation in early 20th-century western Europe that Gramsci developed his complex conceptual apparatus, including *egemonia* (hegemony) and the Integral State.[2] In developing a theoretical language for the workings of organised power under the structural dictates of capital in the interwar years, Gramsci postulated that formal boundaries between 'political society' or 'state', on the one hand, and 'civil society', on the other hand, be conceptualised in dialectical, or boundary-traversing, ways.[3] Gramsci's multi-pronged theoretical arsenal was not devised to make sense of state formation and socio-political forms in Europe's colonies. Still, his dialectical method, dialogical prose and attention to lived realities of uneven development and attendant political-cultural forms lend his theoretical concepts to fertile interrogation of the (post)colonial social formation.[4] In this book, I deploy Gramscian concepts like hegemony and Integral State 'as determinate abstraction[s] that remain linked to concrete historical referents'.[5]

Deciphering 'the political' in Pakistan – and, relatedly, transcending reductive lenses which dominate the mainstream – certainly calls for innovative methodological approaches. To innovate with Gramsci means devoting attention to the banal as much as the spectacular, and to foreground that working people – the most exploited toiling classes as well as those whom I have characterised as driven by middle-class aspiration – inhabit dynamic life worlds. The Gramscian dialectic conjoins analysis of the structural dictates within which political forms are shaped *and* subjective notions of self, community, society, state, and agency.

In the chapters to follow, I will attempt to draw out how political subjects conceive of themselves in the current conjuncture and the agentive practices they engage in accordingly, including in the rapidly expanding digital space. But it is necessary first to explicate the macro and meso level structures of power that condition subjectivation. On the one hand, these structures appear stable and, in fact, highly dynamic in their incorporation of ever-greater populations into circuits of capital, as contractors who seek to garner profits, labouring subjects enabling the generation of surplus, and consumers that facilitate the realisation of profit. On the other hand, these structures are undergirded by the violent dispossession of working masses and expropriation of natural environments, betraying their inherent volatility.

I focus on the exploitation of ethnic peripheries with rich deposits of natural resources as well as the rapid financialisation of land in peri-urban areas to elucidate historical processes of uneven development and how new spatial configurations are being produced in the current conjuncture. Whereas colonial capitalism in its classical incarnation treated the land as a primarily agrarian resource requiring forced settlement of nomadic populations, the development of complementary hydraulic resources and networks of transportation, neoliberalisation has increasingly transformed the land into a financial asset through (sub) urbanisation.

Additionally, previously 'unproductive' regions – especially geo-strategic imperial 'frontiers' subjected to tight territorial control – are now significant sites of accumulation. The 'commons' that represented the primary livelihood source of local communities are being rapidly enclosed by the nexus of state and capital.

Mineral resources deep within the ground or ensconced in mountainous highlands are extracted, while virgin waters and coastlines are appropriated.[6]

The concept of the Integral State facilitates an interrogation of boundary-traversing logics of coercion and consent that undergird contemporary practices of accumulation, and, crucially, their increasingly globalised character. Global supply chains, financial flows, and technological fixes both embody the universalising pretensions of capital, and simultaneously express its fragility, as was so spectacularly demonstrated by the COVID-19 pandemic.

For Gramsci, explaining why working people actively consent to the rules of the game (or defy them) demands an interrogation of histories and geographies of the modern nation-state and wider relations of force.[7] Hegemony in the contemporary period is conditioned by complex circuits of capital linking global and regional capitals to state functionaries, landed classes, big merchant-traders, manufacturers and a plethora of contractors 'from below'. Thus new spatial logics are produced within and beyond the nation-state, even as actual political practice at the micro-level is articulated through deeply-rooted patronage ties. Consequently, practices of accumulation reflect and reproduce entrenched classed, racialised and gendered logics of power.

REPRODUCING THE 'ELITE'

The rupture associated with the global political-economic crisis of 2006–2008 represented the greatest shock to middle-class hegemony in Euro-American societies for a generation. The slogan of the '1% vs the 99%', which was popularised during the Occupy movements, subsequently animated the mass electoral campaigns of Bernie Sanders in the US and Jeremy Corbyn in the UK.

In the Pakistani context, Rosita Armytage posits that the '1%' is both closely integrated with global financial networks and local patronage networks that belie orthodox conceptualisations of capitalism as an impersonal socio-economic order. Her 'ethnography of the micro-politics of elite lives' – the 'elite' defined as those generating more than US$100 million in revenue annually – reveals a secretive but highly insular set of marital and other social networks that bridge traditional categories of class and state power in Pakistan such as civil–military and centre–periphery.[8]

She writes:

> Most of my informants derived the largest proportion of their profits from large-scale industrial projects, many in manufacturing. Others had made their fortunes in developing large-scale infrastructure projects. The enormous profits they have generated have emerged from the opportunities inherent in the classic industrialising society where workers' salaries and political representation are commensurately low. In achieving their high level of profits, many have focused on providing commodities to the domestic market, or on producing high demand export commodities for which they hold a monopoly or equivalent advantage in the world market.[9]

This otherwise useful and intriguing investigation of the 'elite' offers neither specification of the sectors and projects in which these windfall profits are generated, nor elaboration on the exploitative class relations therein. Armytage concurs that capitalist development has brought to the fore newer moneyed classes – what she calls '*navay raje*' – to compete with an 'established *khandaani* elite', the latter with lineages traceable to the colonial educated classes. She further demonstrates how tensions between these dominant factions do not preclude inter-marriages and consolidation of the 1% on the whole. Yet, she also makes the somewhat contradictory assertion that there have been few entrants 'from below' into the ruling coalition over time, suggesting a distinct lack of change within an insular structure of power.

Lyon also presents an argument that accords centrality to kinship ties in the structuring of power relations within society at large. While his empirical focus is rural Punjab, he argues that 'waves of elites' from pre-modern times have been sustained via their inheritance (or what he calls descent) and marriage alliances. In modern Pakistan, both entrenched landed elites and more recent 'industrialist and populist challengers' both rely on and reinforce kinship-based power relations.[10]

More nuanced scholarship about Pakistan's structure of power emphasises that propertied class lineages have evolved alongside social change, particularly urbanisation, and that these lineages are directly connected to the Pakistani military's overarching political, economic, and ideological power.[11]

In contrast to the relatively narrow focus of such work on the structure of power 'from above', a Gramscian exploration of the 'entire complex of practical and theoretical activities' that undergird the dominant hegemonic order demands engagement with everyday articulations of class, ethnic, gendered, caste and state power beyond a narrow 'elite' stratum. This includes investigating practices of often violent accumulation across uneven historical-geographical terrain. Delving into how the state, capital, and other social forces constitute and reproduce the structure of power throws into sharp relief what many scholars proffer to be a ubiquitous logic of kinship ties and unchanging 'cultural norms'.

THE NEW COLONIALISM[12]

> [T]he now indigenous South Asian term 'mafia' is commonly used to refer to business enterprises with political protection that seek to monopolise particular trades, sectors and localities through extra-legal and violent means (as in the 'alcohol mafia', 'water mafia', 'oil mafia', 'coal mafia' or a variety of 'land grabbing' practices by the 'land mafia'). Such syndicates protect clients and cronies and work both against and in tandem with local politicians, the justice system and the bureaucracy.
>
> Michelutti and Harriss-White[13]

The dialectic of state and capital established under European colonial rule in much of Asia and Africa engendered commodification of land, water and forests alongside a proprietary regime objectified as 'rule of law' so that 'ownership' of these said resources was arrogated by the state. There were many modalities through which the latter enfranchised itself and propertied class allies while subjugating indigenous populations. But the emphasis was on creating new forms of a social order based on 'legal' property, further mediated by gradations of caste, tribe, religion and gender.

To establish order often required the use of brute force. Enshrining the 'civilised' practices of commodity production and exchange, the state – and its prized allies – assumed a mandate to engage in 'primitive' accumulation, sanctified by various types of legal exceptionalism.[14] The particular – colonial capitalism – was constitutive of the universal: an imperialised political economy spanning the globe.[15]

The scientific knowledge and requisite technological prowess mobilised by the British Raj facilitated the creation and sustenance of an agrarian economy in the landed plains of Punjab and northern Sindh through the mobilisation of water resources. Far more securitised logics of control were enforced over 'frontier' regions comprising most of contemporary Balochistan and Khyber Pakhtunkhwa.

The Indus Basin region, which became the developed heartland of western India – and later Pakistan – was transformed through perennial irrigation systems and associated mega-infrastructure, constructed by the British from the late 19th century onwards.[16] This agrarian heartland – upstream Punjab far more so than the lower riparian, Sindh – not only became the breadbasket for all of British India, but crucially also became the major recruiting ground for the British Indian Army. As India's main repository of agricultural commodity production, the so-called canal colonies of Punjab were also well-integrated into the global imperial economy fashioned under the Raj. Crucially, this developmental regime was accompanied by the cultivation of widespread consent which explains Punjab's centrality to the hegemonic order in Pakistan.[17]

Whereas a delimited logic of capital was wilfully stimulated in colonial Punjab, territorial imperatives informed statecraft in the non-Punjabi peripheries. Pashtun and Baloch pastoral tribes in northwest India were subjected to various iterations of indirect rule. What ideologues of Empire viewed as 'unruly' subjects unsuited to the modern, civilised world were disciplined through the stick. Meanwhile, 'big men' were offered proverbial carrots, their authority enshrined through the invention of traditional titles and grants of property forthwith. Importantly, pre-British trade flows, particularly the Afghan fruit trade, were not suspended as much as made subordinate to the twin imperatives of hydraulic development and securing Empire's frontier.[18]

These two distinct developmental geographies, and political forms inscribed therein, have not remained static in the decades since formal independence. Major social transformation was engendered by the expanding reach of capital into the developed agrarian heartland from the outset of the Green Revolution (the late 1950s), with further impetus provided by the Gulf migrations, which began in the 1970s. The emergence of small towns and the exponential growth of established metropolitan centres proceeded apace. A declining share of agriculture corresponded to an expanded manufacturing sector in Punjab and, to a lesser extent, Sindh. But the service sector expanded even more rapidly – with self-employment under conditions of so-called 'informality' especially prominent.[19]

In a related vein, emergent political mobilisation – and the hegemonic political order crafted from the late 1970s onwards to counter the left in particular – focused on the intermediate classes that rose to economic prominence as secondary and tertiary sectors of the agrarian economy developed through and with urbanisation.

The non-Punjabi peripheries were also experiencing the growth of an intermediate class – the impetus for which, as I discuss below, was at least partly generated by developmental works initiated by the military government of General Zia ul Haq in the 1980s. Meanwhile, a massive explosion in (largely illicit) economic activity was generated by guerrilla war in Afghanistan, as guns, drugs, and other contraband became big business.[20] Growing numbers of traders, transporters, small manufacturers and even farmers became players in business that extended from the Pak–Afghan border zones to the port city of Karachi. Crucially, the Pakistani military's affiliated corporate arms became central components of this trade.[21]

In subsequent decades, Iranian diesel, cars, cigarettes, juice and even cattle have become important commodities in 'illicit' trade of up to $US5 billion annually that connects Taftan on the Pakistan–Iran border and the Karachi metropolitan area.[22] In the Pashtun border zone with Afghanistan further north, trade of locally grown fruits and nuts, as well as mineral deposits like iron ore, bauxite, and copper has also grown rapidly, with growth in mineral revenues increasing at an eye-catching 35% per annum between 1994–2005.[23]

The deepening of capitalist social relations has thus continued throughout the epoch of neoliberal globalisation, burgeoning opportunities for profiteering spawned by war, mechanisation and the like proceeding apace.

The 'developed' zones of the Indus Basin have become littered with what have been termed 'ruralopolises', largely urbanised belts with the unmistakable imprint of rural-agrarian mores.[24] Industrialisation in Pakistan has been largely limited to agro-processing units like sugar and textiles, which have been conveniently absorbed by the outsourcing practices of multinational conglomerates.[25]

In both big metropolitan centres and smaller towns, large traders and industrialists exercise significant control over markets both for everyday commodities, and, alongside local bureaucrats and a plethora of 'middlemen', mediate access even to basic amenities like water and electricity.[26] Meanwhile, the ethnic peripheries contain islands of 'development', politically savvy intermediate class segments acquiring requisite capital and power necessary to sustain relatively high standards of living.

Neoliberal forms of accumulation have accelerated earlier mercantile flows – often facilitated by mega-infrastructure, and roads most of all – while also ushering in newer and spectacular opportunities for profiteering through the financialisation of land, along with its dialectical other, dispossession. I document presently how swathes of both common and private land in both historical centres and peripheries alike have been bought/forcibly acquired by property developers for gated housing communities. Meanwhile, agricultural-pastoral lands/mountains/forests/water bodies have been appropriated by the nexus of state and capital for 'development'.

The idealised neoliberal developmental regime brings into focus the hegemonic middle-class subject, the primary consumer of 'development', broadly conceived. What Luxemburg conceptualised as capital's incessant impulse to conquer natural economies generates opportunities for brokerage within many intermediate class segments. Those further down the class ladder become footloose labour or survive through variegated forms of self-employment.[27] Either way, the majority of the toiling classes is subject to the logic of capital and the networks of the Integral State.

It is in this sense that the contemporary regime of dispossession can be described as a 'new colonialism' in which, as Fanon posited devastatingly so many decades ago, 'the colonized is elevated beyond his jungle status insofar as he adopts the mother country's cultural standards'.[28] Both intermediate class segments and their consumption hungry 'middle-class' counterparts ascribe to hegemonic logics, cheering on the coercive apparatuses of the state and propping up markets dominated by 'mafias'.

At the apex of this developmental regime is the military. It is both closely integrated into increasingly globalised circuits of capital and heavily imbricated in local political economies. Military personnel and their retainers epitomise the 'art of bossing', which 'refers to the violent, criminal, business, and "democratic" tactics and strategies that some men (seldom women) deploy to control people and resources ... [This] requires a capacity for violence and for making money, repeated acts of give and take, figurations and mythologies'.[29]

Such militarised logics of accumulating power and capital – in Pakistan and many other similar contexts – are nevertheless fraught with contradiction, particularly in the ethnic peripheries, but also in 'developed' centres themselves that are in the throes of a youth bulge. Alongside the other vignettes that I present below, I also bring into focus the economic and political heartland of Punjabi-majority Pakistan, Lahore. The second-largest city in Pakistan boasts the most concentrated segment of young middle-class aspirants for graduation into the 'global village' who at the same time retain loyalty to state-nationalist and dominant religio-cultural mores. I repeat again: the atomised middle-class subject is always on a knife-edge, veering between an insatiable desire for upward mobility and frustration generated by remaining on the outside of the proverbial looking glass. It is on this boundary that potentially transformative political forms can be generated.

REGIMES OF DISPOSSESSION

Many rich empirical studies and attendant theoretical expositions recognise the primacy of coercive power in the *contemporary* rule of capital. Of the many critical engagements with Harvey's seminal concept of 'accumulation by dispossession', Michael Levien offers a productive analytic for the specifically postcolonial condition, namely 'regimes of dispossession', which explicates the 'social relation of coercive redistribution that is organised into socially and historically specific regimes'.[30] Levien's framework is a useful starting point for nuanced interrogation of the various modalities through *and* ends for which the postcolonial state and its class allies have dispossessed the wretched of the earth through time and space.[31]

Levien identifies two major regimes of dispossession. The first lasted from the advent of formal independence until the onset of the neoliberal period. This was the era of high state modernism, featuring public investment in mega-infrastructure such as dams, barrages and mass utilities like electrical power.[32] The hegemonic nation-building project mandated the dispossession of certain segments of the population in the name of the 'greater common good', resistance generally cast off and/or disciplined under the pretext that it was 'anti-development'.

However, with the end of state-led developmentalism and the ascendance of neoliberal orthodoxy, a new regime of dispossession was inaugurated. In this (contemporary) historical period, the 'land broker state' merely facilitates multinational companies and their local dependents in the acquisition of land in rural and peri-urban areas.

In contrast to state-led developmentalism of a bygone era, Lieven insists that the contemporary regime of dispossession is not motivated by the imperative of 'development', notwithstanding the lofty promises made to the dispossessed. I disagree. The signifier of 'development' remains a major pillar of the contemporary hegemonic order. To be precise, both the state-led regime of dispossession and its neoliberal successor transfer(red) the burden of 'development' onto largely invisibilised – and in the most extreme cases, criminalised – populations.[33]

Since the turn of the millennium, Pakistan has experienced a spurt in mega infrastructural investment sustained by the state borrowing vast amounts of money from the IFIs, and more recently from China under the latter's Belt and Road Initiative (BRI). As I will demonstrate presently, the state's collaboration with global creditors to build roads, ports, power plants as well as extract the natural resources necessary for 'development' has engendered significant dispossession.[34]

These projects are designed and executed through the proverbial 'public–private partnership' or what one critical scholar calls the 'new developmentalism'.[35] Notwithstanding claims of both state and capital about the universal benefits of neoliberal development, the evidence confirms that the hegemonic developmental regime actually deepens class, caste and other entrenched hierarchies.

LAND AS ASSET

> While land has always been a political–economic asset in rural Pakistan, today it is increasingly desired by domestic and international capital looking to build mega-residential enclaves, shopping complexes, education cities, and various types of infrastructures through public–private partnerships. In this new frontier of capitalist development, myriad small and large-scale land transactions involving village landlords, state officials, brokers and real estate developers push the cycle of land acquisitions deeper and deeper into the periphery.
>
> Nausheen H. Anwar[36]

The gated housing community is arguably the archetype of neoliberal developmental imaginaries in contemporary South Asia and Sub Saharan Africa. Within walled ghettos are not only ideal-type constructed homes for the ideal-type 'middle-class' nuclear family but also a plethora of assorted services, including shopping malls, pristinely manicured lawns and parks (even where the surrounding ecosystem is arid), air-conditioned cinemas and bowling alleys, as well as places of religious worship. Security guards litter well-ordered streets and enforce strict entry and exit rules. By all accounts, home ownership in such gated communities constitutes a major pillar of contemporary middle-class aspiration.[37]

The rapidity with which the (sub)urban landscape has come to be dotted with such housing schemes in much of the postcolonial non-western world speaks to the immensely profitable, albeit volatile nature of 'hot capital' asset bubbles. The residential real estate market is now the world's single most profitable outlet for moving capital, its value estimated at US$217 trillion.[38] Capital's insatiable appetite for expansion inevitably produces immiseration. 'Private territories and gated communities in Southern cities … creat[e] exclusionary spaces, increasing residential segregation, restrict … freedom of movement, and exacerbat[e] social divides'.[39]

In Pakistan, gated housing communities are proliferating across both 'developed' and 'underdeveloped' geographical zones, and reflect how capital produces space in increasingly uniform ways across historically distinct social-spatial formations. State functionaries – and military intermediaries most of all – are central to this economic and political project, lending weight to the imaginary of the Integral State.

Gwadar, Balochistan

Historically, Balochistan is the most brutalised of all of Pakistan's ethnic peripheries, and also a site of multi-scalar 'developmental' interventions championed by Pakistan's militarised state apparatus alongside various fractions of local and global capital.[40] Arguably the crown jewel of the US$62bn China–Pakistan Economic Corridor (CPEC) is the deep-sea port at Gwadar on the south-western tip of Balochistan.[41] The Baloch national question is more acute than all of Pakistan's other oppressed ethnic nations; in 2004, the fifth armed insurgency led by Baloch nationalists against the Pakistani state was triggered by a series of events which included the initiation of port construction in Gwadar.[42]

Prior to its quite dramatic discursive entry into mainstream Pakistani lexicon as the 'new Dubai', Gwadar was a small settlement largely comprised of subsistence fishing communities, an estimated 90% of the population reliant on the fisheries sector for livelihoods.[43] In two decades since Gwadar Port construction began, the entire political economy of the settlement and coastal region at large has been transformed, not to mention cultural mores, spatial make-up and ethnic constitution.

On the one hand, indigenous fisherfolk have been displaced from their homes and livelihoods, their only compensation the grant of often shoddy residential plots in ghettoised sectors of the emergent city. In their place, corporate trawlers, both foreign and domestic, have come to dominate the fisheries sector.[44] On the other hand, a plethora of proverbial gold hunters have descended upon Gwadar – and indeed on the entire 600 km coastline stretching to Karachi – to generate windfall profits from the sale and purchase of real estate.

To be sure, an unprecedented economic upheaval has taken place on the Makkuran coast in the past two decades, centring around the metamorphosis of land into a financial asset. The Makkuran Coastal Highway was built in 2004 to facilitate access from the country's financial centre, Karachi, to the three coastal towns of Pasni, Ormara and Gwadar. Beaches and virgin lands along the route thus became available for up-country tourists and profiteers alike to make merry. The collusion of local influentials with Chinese construction companies and real estate moguls to 'develop' the coastline have led to both unbridled accumulation and dispossession.

Somewhat astonishingly for a deep-sea port that has been pitched as a competitor to Dubai, Gwadar has only intermittent access to electricity, much of which is supplied from the Iranian side of the border.[45] It was only in 2006 that much of the land in and around the Makkuran Coastal Highway was actually codified and 'settled', a process in which bureaucrats and property developers made windfall profits by enclosing common lands. Available statistics in 2017 suggested that 20,000 acres of land were yet to be settled across Gwadar district, confirming an ongoing gold rush to the exclusion of locals without power and influence.[46] It is emblematic that local Gwadaris comprise less than 3% of the residents of the two original housing schemes completed in the early 2000s.

The military is at the forefront of an almost limitless land grab in Gwadar and surrounding districts. All three of the services – the army, air force and navy – have acquired tens of thousands of acres of land, both along the coastline, and hundreds of kilometres inland. This includes 80,000 acres of forest land in the otherwise protected Hingol National Park in Lasbela district and a reported 45,000 acres of land for a garrison close to Gwadar city.[47] Naturally, when the military gets involved, civil bureaucrats vested with inordinate power to 'settle' land go out of their way to override already flimsy legalities of land acquisition, while also running roughshod over the limited monetary compensation to which indigenous communities are entitled.[48]

The imperative of 'security' for CPEC, and 'development' more broadly, is a *carte blanche* for all such land grabs. In late 2020 a brazen announcement was made that a fence would be built to bifurcate Gwadar, ostensibly to secure installations and infrastructure, as well as Chinese engineers and construction workers active in and around the city. According to the chairman of the Gwadar Port Authority (GPA), 'Gwadar area is *brimming* with a number of security check posts. Escorting conveys with high-level surveillance are definitely good for safety (italics mine)'.[49]

A *jirga* (public meeting) of political parties, civil society organisations and community elders held in Gwadar on 27 December 2020 to deliberate on the fencing project effectively became a parley of local real estate developers to lobby furiously to have their own projects included within the fenced area. In effect, Gwadar's 'development' is a race to become a part of the militarised accumulation regime, if even for scraps. The choice facing even small-time operators is to accede to imperatives of the emergent elite ghetto or be disposed into the dustbin of history alongside indigenous communities considered surplus to the requirements of capital.

Bahria Town Karachi-Hyderabad

I now move on to a less remote periphery that has been enveloped by one of the biggest real estate schemes in Pakistan. The planned gated community of Bahria Town Karachi is spread out across more than 30,000 acres and is swallowing up what has been called the 'agrarian–urban' frontier of the city.[50] The coastal metropolis, Pakistan's biggest city with a population of 25 million, is linked to Sindh province's second-biggest city, Hyderabad, by a 160 km eight-lane highway that originates at Karachi's northernmost tip. For almost 20 km of this journey, a massive sprawling elite ghetto litters the landscape towards the west, literally flattening everything that comes in its path.

Bahria Town Karachi was inaugurated in 2014, and will be home, the company's boasts, to a million residents upon completion in 2022. It promises the third biggest mosque in the world, a 36-hole golf course and a plethora of commercial and recreational facilities behind heavily fortified walls. Less advertised is the expropriation of at least 150 *goths* (villages) and an estimated 40,000 indigenous people through systematic and often violent land grabs, with the connivance of civilian and paramilitary state personnel.

The barely disguised thuggery has been taken up at the highest level by the Supreme Court (SC) of Pakistan, which heard numerous petitions between 2016 and 2019 against the illegality of land allotments made to Bahria Town Karachi by the Malir Development Authority (MDA), the government agency with jurisdiction over the area within which the scheme falls.[51] However, in what was a quite stunning admission about the nexus of state and capital, the SC ruled that Bahria Town could retain and in fact establish legal authority over the disputed land in exchange for a negotiated sum of money, reportedly Rs. 460 billion.

The precedent set by the Supreme Court to *post-facto* whitewash all coercive land acquisition practices makes clear that Bahria Town, like all big real estate developers, enjoys substantial influence at the highest echelons of state power in Pakistan and beyond.[52] This was underlined in even more spectacular fashion by a £190 million property settlement in the UK that allowed Bahria Town head Malik Riaz to transfer sufficient monies back to Pakistan so as to pay the Supreme Court the stipulated sum. The UK transactions, which involved property owned by former Prime Minister Nawaz Sharif, came to fruition after the Pakistani state intervened to request that the UK's National Crime Agency (NCA) halt an investigation into Malik Riaz's affairs.[53]

Crucially, this influence is matched at the local level by a nexus of power involving civilian administrators, real estate agents, pro-company residents of the affected villages, as well as the military and paramilitary institutions operating both in formal and illicit guises. Bahria Town's acquisition of local lands takes place through a combination of strong-arm tactics and collusion with local *patwaris* (revenue collectors), the latter tampering with land records to sanctify the forced dispossession of local villagers.

As in Gwadar, progressive political activists, lawyers, and members of the local community have bravely resisted these land grabs despite sometimes intense repression.[54] But this has not halted the tidal wave of dispossession, as most villagers ultimately accede to some financial compensation rather than face violence and ongoing harassment. While some swallow the bitter pill of being forced off their lands and permanent displacement from their historical livelihoods, others position themselves as beneficiaries by playing the role of junior partners with the nexus of profiteers. Local collaborators are rewarded with plots within Bahria Town. Others are more ambitious and invest cash from their exploits as goons into speculative real estate investments elsewhere in Karachi or, indeed, further along the Karachi-Hyderabad expressway. As Levien notes in his Indian case study:

> [T]he formulation of accumulation by dispossession as a phenomenon that pits capital versus the peasantry (or 'commoners') is overly simplistic ... The rampant real estate speculation that swept through the villages ... in which dispossessed farmers were given a small stake by the neoliberal compensation model – produced not a singular 'neo-rentier' class ... but a chain of rentiership in which speculative opportunities were unevenly exploited by those (men) with different endowments of economic, social, and cultural capital.[55]

The regime of dispossession in the agrarian–urban frontier of Karachi produces a not dissimilar subjectivity amongst local villagers. Real estate development can be experienced as an opportunity for those with better means, but there is nevertheless a very real danger of losing everything due to violent dispossession. In any case, hegemonic common sense encourages those who have even the slightest opportunity to lay claim to membership in the 'chain of rentiership'. That the majority of villagers do not have such opportunities and are displaced entirely from livelihoods confirms only the ruthless nature of the survival-of-the-fittest mentality that undergirds the politics of fear and desire.

DHA Lahore

Long before Bahria emerged as the preeminent name in the burgeoning real estate market, acquisition of a plot in Defence Housing Authority (DHA) was the primary embodiment of middle-class aspiration. From the 1980s, 'through the power of the army, the DHA and its affiliated cantonments [became] major players in land politics, leading to land and property speculation for and by the elite'.[56]

Karachi's DHA was the original prototype. Inaugurated as Defence Housing Society, the scheme engendered significant spatial transformation, with land reclamation of the city's coastline facilitating its expansion over time. DHA Lahore, which I document presently, has, since 2001, enveloped more than 25,000 acres of agricultural land on the eastern outskirts of the city. What one critical scholar has called 'military enclosures' allow for small village spaces to be retained within DHA; in effect, most villagers are eventually expropriated through both the market and outright coercion.[57]

The planned grids, commercial spaces, parks and roads that are so attractive to the idealised middle-class subject represent 'infrastructures of war' that slowly but surely subsume village properties, cemeteries, houses, mosques, swamps, graveyards and schools.[58] Where villagers have resisted 'civilised' attempts to acquire their lands, walls have been erected by the DHA administration to effectively ghettoise the affected villages. Once they are literally pushed against the wall, villagers are obliged to sell their land.

A handful of bigger villages have managed to ward off complete annihilation due to sustained resistance in the face of violent dispossession, which the DHA administration has undertaken with impunity. Ultimately, however, these 'peri-urban conglomerations' end up as 'surveilled and controlled open-air encampments'.[59] Not only are they subject to spatial strangulation, but their livelihood options are all but reduced to domestic service and/or other forms of precarious wage/self-employed labour. Among other things, this forced transformation leads to many women entering the labour market, mostly as domestic servants in DHA's mansions.

Like in the other case studies, DHA Lahore's still ongoing expansion produces a chain of rentiership. Village communities prior to DHA's advent were hardly egalitarian *per se*; in some instances, landowning classes have benefited from the sale of their land to DHA by purchasing plots within the new gated community or investing their newfound wealth elsewhere. In contrast landless classes and artisanal castes become part of the already massive urban informal workforce, producing yet another 'surplus population'.

The crux of the matter, of course, is the demand for plots in DHA; this demand drives the dispossession of villagers. Urban metropoles like Lahore are decisive cauldrons in the contradictory mosaic of militarised Pakistani capitalism. Insofar as millions of young Punjabis seeking upward mobility – symbolised by the membership of the gated communities like DHA – continue to believe in the promises of the neoliberal developmental regime, the mandate to dispossess the proverbial villager will remain unchallenged.

A universalist politics against dispossession and for an alternative imaginary of development across uneven historical-geographical terrain must, in the final analysis, have meaningful roots amongst Punjab's middle-class subject. Future generations of Punjabis will, after all, bear the brunt of ecological breakdown that is being hastened by neoliberal development as heavily as their non-Punjabi peers.

FROM WORLDMAKING TO NEOLIBERAL 'DEVELOPMENT'

In the immediate post-independence conjuncture, the technological means for capital to pillage natural resources across the length and breadth of the social formation – and indeed, world – were far less advanced than they are today. Alongside such structural constraints, distinct ideological and political imperatives were also at play. Most notably:

> Anticolonial nationalists refigured decolonization as a radical rupture – one that required a wholesale transformation of the colonized and a reconstitution of the international order. Accordingly, it can be reasonably argued that anticolonial nationalists [were] worldmakers rather than solely nation builders.[60]

The grand political horizon of remaking the world receded from the late 1970s, giving way to the earliest incarnations of what became the hegemonic neoliberal order. The New International Economic Order (NIEO) spearheaded by the so-called

G77 countries was, in effect, the last hurrah before the regimes of Reagan, Thatcher, Pinochet, Zia ul Haq and many others made common cause to 'rollback' whatever gains the internationalist movement had made.

Chile is often described as the world's neoliberal laboratory, where the notorious 'Chicago Boys' spearheaded a massive recalibration of economic priorities and unleashed the moniker that would become known as the 'free market'.[61] Pinochet's contemporary in Pakistan, General Zia ul Haq, came to global prominence for his service to the 'free world' through decidedly different means. Pakistan was the staging ground of the so-called *jihad* against the Soviet Union, an imperialist war-making project which continues to play out in Pakistan, Afghanistan and the region at large till this day.

As significant to the future political economy of Pakistan was the developmental project inaugurated during the Zia years.[62] While the military junta presided over broader policy shifts associated with structural adjustment policies – privatisation, trade and financial liberalisation, and steady reduction in pro-poor subsidies – it did not 'denationalis[e] in haste'. Given that 'ownership and control of public sector industries was an effective tool for granting political patronage and favour', there was no reason to 'gift such means away'.[63]

The Zia government facilitated a greatly enhanced military footprint over Pakistan's political economy. Real estate, as I have already discussed above, has since become a favourite destination of military capital, or what the primary chronicler of the military's corporate empire, Ayesha Siddiqa, has termed 'milbus'.[64] However, no less important was the extension of military business enterprise into infrastructure and logistics. The Frontier Works Organisation (FWO), which was founded in 1966, and the National Logistics Cell (NLC), created in 1982, are today the country's biggest players in infrastructural development.[65]

The Zia government initiated a long-term project of road-building in, and enhancing 'connectivity' to, the country's geographical peripheries. A 'massive expansion in road transport infrastructure' began in 1982, with the peripheries of Azad Kashmir, Northern Areas (now Gilgit-Baltistan), and the Federally Administered Tribal Areas (now merged into Khyber Pakhtunkhwa) explicitly prioritised.[66]

Almost four decades later, the Zia regime's political-economic project has metamorphosed into a militarised regime of dispossession that holds sway under the pretext of 'development'.[67] I noted earlier that Levien's neat separation of past and present regimes of dispossession into state-led and private sector-led respectively is too simplistic; the cases I document below are 'mega' development projects operationalised by the neoliberal 'public–private partnership'.

Neoliberal development is generating unprecedented pressures on natural ecosystems through the expropriation of hitherto untapped resources. While the most acute ecological pressures are being exerted in the geographical peripheries, the developmental regime does not spare ecosystems within historical centres either. Many mega projects – including road-building – are part of the vaunted CPEC initiative, signalling both what a prospective Chinese-dominated global order will look like and the vision of 'development' that drives it.[68]

Thar, Sindh

Thar is an arid desert region that is notable for being one of Pakistan's most 'underdeveloped' peripheries. On Pakistan's easternmost border with 'arch-enemy' India, Thar is one of the most heavily securitised parts of the country. It was a major staging ground of both the 1965 and 1971 Indo-Pak wars, Pakistan seizing Thari territory previously held by India in 1965 and India then returning the favour in 1971. Accordingly, Pakistani officialdom's dealings in the region are imbued with what has been termed a deep 'cartographic anxiety'.[69] That Thar is the only Hindu-majority region in Pakistan renders Tharis even more suspicious in the official mind.

Remarkably, the first major black-top road was built in Thar in 1987 as part of the larger state-led effort to 'integrate' geographical peripheries. In the intervening three decades, the region has undergone a degree of urbanisation as secondary and tertiary sectors of a largely agro-pastroral economy – dominated by livestock – have grown. At the turn of the century, Thar exploded into Pakistani mainstream consciousness when the mining of massive coal deposits, first 'discovered' in the early 1990s, began in earnest. A 259 km road to facilitate extraction from the coalfields linking Thar and its two major towns of Mithi and Islamkot to Karachi was completed in 2015, confirming the centrality of road-building to projects in which 'borderland locations are transformed from marginal places to areas of resource extraction'.[70]

At approximately 175 billion tonnes, Thar's coalfields represent the world's 7th biggest reserve. The extraction of Thar's coal has been depicted within Pakistan as a home-grown panacea for the country's growing energy needs; the Pakistani mainstream became exposed to the fact of Thar's vast deposits in the mid-2000s when chronic power shortages were afflicting many metropolitan centres.

Production from Thar's coal mines began in late 2019, by which time the project had already caused the displacement of local communities and started transforming the ecosystem of the region at large. More than 9000 square miles of Thar's total area of 22,000 square miles will be mined for coal, while the rest will be subject to substantial damming, affecting all of the region's 150,000 people. The Sindh Engro Coal Mining Company (SECMC) – which is managing the project alongside China Power International – has predictably engaged in standard corporate-speak about the benefits of 'development' to local communities. Yet, the company's hiring and related policies have to date only entrenched caste and religious hierarchies in Thar.

Meanwhile, dispossession – or 'involuntary land acquisition' in the language of some experts – proceeds apace. In one of the earliest villages to be affected, 1500 acres of land was taken from local residents in return for the paltry amount of Rs. 100,000 per acre. Negotiations to increase compensation did not benefit all displaced landowners equally: in Thar too, a complex 'chain of rentiership' is evident, those of high social and economic status inevitably garnering a greater share of the relatively meagre spoils that the dominant state-capital nexus allows to trickle down the patronage chain. The social status of low-caste, predominantly Hindu villagers who did not possess land to begin with, has meanwhile worsened.

Organised resistance to dispossession has, to date, been restricted to the village of Ghorano, which has borne the brunt of the construction of a 2700 acre reservoir to collect effluent from the coal extraction process. The protest movement spread as far as Sindh's major urban centres of Karachi and Hyderabad, and was broadly supported by the Sindhi nationalist intelligentsia. But repression by the state's security apparatus and the gradual isolation of scheduled caste Meghwars who led the protests led to the movement eventually subsiding.[71]

The approximately 5000 residents of Ghorano lost most of their land, with only those having made 'compromises' with the authorities gaining some compensation in the process. Khan captures the politics of fear and desire in Thar incisively: '"[C]onsent" is produced through an everyday acceptance of a cultural ideology of "development" even in the face of circumstances such as the uneven gains and displacement of population'.[72]

The reproduction of caste, class and religious difference in Thar through the prevalent regime of dispossession can be expected to play out into the foreseeable future. The devastating ecological effects of coal mining are now well established around the world, but Thar's indigenous peoples will nevertheless continue bearing its costs in the name of 'national security' and 'development'. Indeed, local ecosystems are already in a state of disrepair: to take only one example, more than 70% of Thar's people have no access to clean drinking water, and if the mining of coal continues unabated, already contaminated saline water will effectively become poisonous. As drought-like conditions intensify due to climate change, the perversity of Thar's depiction as a haven of 'development' becomes even more galling.

Gilgit-Baltistan

Gilgit-Baltistan (GB) is a unique territorial space emblematic of the contemporary hegemonic order in Pakistan. A liminal zone of exception whose residents remain deprived of basic constitutional rights, GB borders China at Pakistan's northernmost tip. It functions both as a buffer for trade and connectivity as well as 'a site … for nationalist valorizations of its "natural beauty", as well as international desires for rendering it a pristine natural area'.[73]

GB is primarily represented in the Pakistani mainstream as a tourist haven at the crossroads of the Himalayan, Hindu-Kush and Karakoram mountain ranges. Millions of down-country Pakistanis visit the region annually, the local economy depending significantly on tourist revenues, particularly in the summer months. In this sense alone, the popular imagination of GB epitomises the neoliberal developmental regime.

CPEC in fact represents the latest and most significant intervention to incorporate the region into Pakistan's economic and political ambit – even though the region's 2 million people remain disenfranchised – while connecting it to its primary developmental patron, China. Sino–Pak infrastructural cooperation was christened by the Karakoram Highway (KKH), completed in 1976. The construction of the KKH not only linked the mainstream to a previously 'remote' and 'underdeveloped' geographical periphery, but also underlined how the business of road-building in, and extension of other infrastructure to, a geographical periphery, accords power, resources and legitimacy to military-controlled entities like FWO and NLC.

During the Zia years, private commerce was inaugurated on the KKH, replacing barter. Another watershed was the operationalisation in 2005 of a dry port at Sost, 75 km from the Pak–China border – control of Sost was eventually handed over to the NLC in 2016. Seen thus, CPEC marks the culmination of a steady scaling-up of connectivity and accumulation such that 'investment and finance, privatisation, and securitisation converge under a neoliberal administrative framework'.[74]

Aside from road-building, one of CPEC's major infrastructural pillars is the laying of a countrywide fibre-optic cable, which will both transform Pakistan's communication network and give China extensive control over information flows in the country. China Mobile already accounts for 20% of domestic telecommunications traffic, and this share is projected to increase dramatically in the near future. While there are other competitors to China Mobile in the telecommunications market in down-country Pakistan, the military-run Special Communications Organization (SCO) enjoys a virtual monopoly over cell phone and internet services in GB itself.

Similar to other previously 'remote' geographical peripheries that I have documented here, dispossession stalks development in GB as its dialectical other. Local traders that previously eked out small margins are being squeezed by both entrepreneurs from metropolitan Pakistan and China. More generally, GB's people are migrating out of the region in larger numbers than ever, due both to the insularity of an unrepresentative colonial bureaucracy populated largely by down-country Pakistanis, as well as the capture by 'outsiders' of CPEC-generated accumulation opportunities.[75]

Mineral extraction has intensified dramatically since the turn of the century.[76] Taking advantage of prevailing legal-administrative lacunae, down-country civil and military bureaucrats, along with toothless GB government officials have issued hundreds of leases to mine gold, copper, bauxite, marble and other stones. Chinese companies are increasingly prominent in the mining sector, sometimes partnering with Pashtun and Punjabi contractors, although the latter operate independently as well. Much of the business in this sector, as ever, flows through the FWO and NLC.

GB's glaciers and glacial lakes are the lifeblood of Pakistan's river system, and are now warming at rates higher than the rest of the country, with increasingly disruptive effects. Landsliding is increasingly common; one such incident in 2010 near the village of Attabad in upper Hunza killed 19 and created a 22 km reservoir which displaced thousands, blocking the KKH for months. A campaign demanding compensation for affectees led by a local son of the soil, Baba Jan, became a full-fledged political movement that garnered the support of large swathes of GB's youth. The state's response was to jail Baba Jan on trumped-up murder charges for almost a decade.[77]

The dominant developmental regime has largely subsumed dissenting voices in GB. The Integral State is sustained by loyal subjects who seek incorporation into the dominant developmental regimes, as marginal traders, translators for Chinese patrons, sub-contractors for big economic players like the FWO, SCO and NLC, and, indeed, as state functionaries.

During the Musharraf dictatorship, GB's youth were inducted into the various military institutions in larger numbers than ever. Many served in military expeditions conducted in Pashtun regions like Waziristan at the height of the 'war on terror', a subject to which I turn in the next chapter. '[L]ocal employment in the military and sustained participation in security operations has produced a political economy of feelings that cultivates honor, pride, and loyalty toward the military, and hence, toward a military-state'.[78]

Making one peripheral region's subaltern subjects the face of the state's coercive power against another periphery is, in no uncertain terms, a distinctive modality of colonial statecraft. More generally, successive middle-class hegemonies in Pakistan have been sustained by uneven developmental logics that divide historical centres and peripheries. It is only by bridging this divide that an alternative hegemonic conception to the dialectic of fear and desire can be fomented.

This brings me back to Lahore.

The city on the River Ravi

As grand developmental projects to fuel the neoliberal imagination go, the Ravi Riverfront Urban Development Project trumps all. An almost fantastical scheme on the banks of the Ravi River on the northern outskirts of metropolitan Lahore, the project envisions the construction of a planned city over a period of 30 years, catering to a population in excess of 10 million spread out over more than 100,000 acres of land. On paper, this would make it the second-biggest planned city in Pakistan, after the federal capital Islamabad.[79] The project ostensibly caters to organic demand for 'development' that is unattainable within Lahore's existing spatial make-up. To be sure, the project's stipulated purpose is to ameliorate population pressure, and regenerate exhausted ecosystems.

A dubious Environmental Impact Assessment (EIA) report commissioned by the government in 2019 served the purpose of 'green-washing' the subsumption of 80,000 acres of arable agricultural land and irreparable loss of flora, fauna and existing habitats.[80] The claims of planners that the project will facilitate regeneration of the Ravi River and its tributary ecosystems along the 46 km of planned project construction are completely outlandish. Water flows in the Ravi Basin have been nominal for decades; the river originates in neighbouring India, its control accorded to the latter under the terms of the 1960 Indus Water Treaty. The project envisages the building of three barrages to artificially maintain water levels in and around Lahore city, as well as a link canal to transfer water from the Chenab River to the west. Aside from the impact of such damming, how the transfer of water away from the Chenab will affect farming in agricultural plains further west is unspecified.

The construction of wastewater treatment plants is also projected to contribute to sustainable water flows. Over the past two decades, the quality of water in the Ravi has deteriorated so much that the river can now effectively be considered a sewage drain. It is noteworthy that no Pakistani governing regime has hitherto constructed wastewater treatment plants to serve working-class residents living in the inner city near the Ravi.

The announcement of the project engendered an immediate backlash from the thousands of farming families whose lands will be forcibly acquired for the project. Yet the portents are clear; as with so many other such 'developmental' projects, colonial statutes like the 1894 Land Acquisition Act are being mobilised to steamroll any meaningful resistance. A governmental body with extraordinary powers, the Ravi Urban Development Authority (RUDA), has been incorporated to see the project to fruition. While there may yet be not insignificant resistance to the project – some was initially triggered by a 'public consultation' as part of the EIA – combinations of coercion and financial compensation similar to the other 'developmental' projects I have documented in the vignettes above will likely also clear the way for project execution in this case.

For there to be a different outcome would require a critical mass of resistance to the project beyond those being dispossessed. If the city on the River Ravi does eventually come into being, will most Lahoris that constitute the captive market for it actually be able to gain membership of it? Or will it become yet another outlet for speculative capital, and in the process exclude the vast majority of middle-class aspirants? There is little prospect of such critical interrogation in the mediatised glare of the hegemonic fear and desire.

At the current rate of environmental degradation, the trials and tribulations that today's youth will face in their middle-age is impossible to predict. But the trends are clear. Lahore is already one of the world's most polluted cities, its air quality index (AQI) in excess of liveable levels for most of the winter months due to endemic slash and burn farming, emissions and elite consumption, and waste-disposal practices.[81]

The wretched of the earth, including surplus populations forced to migrate to metropolitan Pakistan from the hinterland, will inevitably continue to bear the brunt of ecological meltdown. But there is little to suggest that the millions of Punjabis that both for historical and contemporary reasons constitute the consenting critical mass of the contemporary hegemonic regime will be able to insulate themselves in elite ghettos with access to all of the amenities for a 'good life'.

It is this critical mass – inclusive of other captive subjects in metropolitan Pakistan – whose political agency will, in my opinion, determine the fate of the politics of fear and desire. It can consciously or otherwise continue to provide a mandate for historical and contemporary logics of uneven development and colonial statecraft, or it can choose to put in its lot, over the due course of time, with a universalist imaginary beyond dispossession, covetousness, militarism and ecological breakdown.

Sooner rather than later, all will have to confront Marx's insight:

> Even a whole society, a nation, or even all simultaneously existing societies together, are not the owners of the globe. They are only its possessors, its usufructuaries, and like *boni patres familias* [good fathers of families] they must hand it down to succeeding generations in an improved condition.[82]

2
Fear and desire

> The profound hypocrisy and inherent barbarism of bourgeois civilisation lies unveiled before our eyes, turning from its home, where it assumes respectable forms, to the colonies, where it goes naked.
>
> Karl Marx, 1853

It is axiomatic that contemporary regimes of dispossession breed polarisation. The class and other social divides that have grown under the regime of neoliberal globalisation, however, are increasingly obfuscated in the intellectual, political and media mainstream around the world. Greater disclosure about the brutalising realities of the global political economy become unavoidable during exceptional moments – the initial weeks after the novel coronavirus was declared a global pandemic an apt example – but the crisis-ridden hegemonic order nevertheless survives and thrives through a combination of fictions founded upon commodity fetishism and hate.

In this chapter, I tease out how the universalising tendencies of capital have necessitated an intensification of colonial logics of racialised, gendered and classed power in Pakistan. The hegemonic apparatus has gone into literal and figurative overdrive to generate consent for the prevailing developmental regime.

Triumphalist discourses about neoliberal globalisation receded in western countries following the political-economic ruptures of 2006–2008, culminating in the rise of reactionaries championing xenophobic nationalism. In the postcolonial world, however, neoliberal ideological signifiers continued to be largely unchallenged, alongside the paraphernalia of the so-called 'war on terror'. Taking forward insights from the previous chapter, I demonstrate presently that the dialectic of 'development' and 'terrorism' undergirds the politics of fear and desire. A combination of coercion and majoritarian consent facilitates the expansionary logic of capital on the one hand, and criminalises resistance and embryonic progressive alternatives on the other hand.

The analytic of the Integral State brought into focus contemporary regimes of dispossession that reflect both historical continuities as well as spatial reconfigurations in the interplay of state and capital under (post)colonial conditions. In this sense, the current conjuncture can be distinguished from a bygone era when political subjects and hegemonic forms corresponded to different temporal and spatial frames. Uneven development and colonial statecraft nevertheless reinforce Marx's classical formulation about 'town' and 'country'. If the town is occupied by civilised elements seeking peaceful 'development', then the country is a suspect, otherwise remote place inhabited at best by unruly, backward elements, and at worst by threats to society, the most threatening of which are cast off as 'terrorists'.[1]

By town I refer primarily to urban conglomerations but also include more variegated geographies; the suburban gated housing community offers the imaginary of a 'town' sheltered from the excesses of metropolitan life. In a similar vein, country refers primarily to the classic rural hinterland – distinct both for its physical remoteness and natural resources – but figuratively also harkens to metropolitan settings inhabited by surplus populations both past and present; the paradigmatic example is slums and squatter settlements. The latter are home to racial/caste/ethnic communities wilfully extorted and/or criminalised by the formal state, propertied classes and xenophobic majoritarian social forces more generally.

Town and country are far from insular entities, and middle-class aspiration serves precisely the purpose of generating consent from wilful elements within the country who seek to graduate into the town. Yet, hegemony, as Gramsci reminds us, is never a sealed, hermeneutic fact, and the contemporary youth bulge throws up tens of millions whose desire for credentials, livelihoods and dignity if not met, or worse yet shattered, represent a volatile chink in the proverbial armour. Where the hegemonic apparatus – media, formal education, the workplace, religious institutions and the like – fails to generate consent for the combination of 'development' and the imperative of defeating 'terrorism', dissidents can coalesce around alternative political ideas.

THE SOCIAL BASE OF REACTIONARY FORCES

The future trajectory of middle-class aspiration will be conditioned by three interrelated structuring forces. Two of these are specific to the postcolonial societies of South Asia and Sub Saharan Africa, namely a youth bulge and the distinct form of capitalism in which a large percentage of the workforce is engaged in tenuous self-employment and/or subject to extremely exploitative and precarious forms of wage labour. The third is the rapid digitalisation of social life. In sum, a rapidly growing number of young people inhabit a lifeworld enabled by digital technology, yet do not necessarily possess the material means – the money commodity and thereby others – to become comfortably 'middle class'.[2]

Digitalisation has in fact facilitated the emergence of a semi-autonomous field of politics in which new logics of power are (re)produced, alongside the entrenched patronage networks that have historically conditioned hegemony. As a rule, young people dominate these emergent digitalised networks of 'the political'.

Here I examine the Pakistan Tehrik-e-Insaf (PTI) as a vehicle of the youthful, middle-class subject disillusioned with 'democratic' institutions of mass representation in the neoliberal present. The experience of the PTI can be extrapolated to many parallel postcolonial contexts where a youthful and digitally connected demographic imbued with the middle-class aspiration forms the vocal support base of a reactionary coalition that claims to break the monopoly of 'dominant elites'. In fact, the reactionary coalition is heavily reliant on entrenched networks of patronage that undergird political, financial and religious establishments.[3]

I noted in the introductory chapter how the neoliberal developmental regime inaugurated by the dictatorship of General Pervez Musharraf spawned an idealised middle-class subject that subsequently became the motor force of the PTI. Following Musharraf's ouster in 2008, an already substantial cult of personality around Imran Khan metamorphosed into an establishment-backed political coalition that eventually acquired governmental power in 2018.

In its genesis, the PTI brought together Imran Khan's considerable network of personal admirers, particularly amongst relatively affluent members of the Pakistani diaspora. The latter contributed generously from the late 1980s to Khan's cancer hospital initiative – his commitment to charity buttressed his mystique amongst socially liberal segments with an avowed distaste for politics and an already established penchant for supporting messiahs in the mould of the colonial educated classes. Imran Khan himself writes in one of his many self-congratulatory autobiographies:

> My experience founding a hospital [taught] me a great deal about my fellow countrymen and myself. I saw the true potential of ordinary Pakistani people ... I was drawing closer still to the idea of trying to help Pakistan politically. Besides, in challenging the status quo, and trying to fill a social security void left by a succession of Pakistani leaders, I found myself dragged into politics, whether I liked it or not.[4]

In due course, Imran Khan's personality cult enveloped younger generations too. The fledgling PTI became the first political party in Pakistan to digitise both its recruitment process as well as its public message, boasting 10 million members both within Pakistan and across the global diaspora by 2013. An insider who later departed the fold described it as a catch-all 'social movement' which attracted otherwise dormant political subjects from within the 'urban middle-class ... who had never before voted and who had always seen politics as a dangerous and futile endeavour' especially within the context of Pakistan's constituency-based, patronage-heavy electoral system.[5]

To take but one example: women and girls from relatively affluent backgrounds were given access to Pakistan's otherwise heavily male-dominated public sphere through PTI's public rallies, thereby confirming the lineage between Imran Khan's government-in-waiting and General Pervez Musharraf's regime; both boasted overwhelming support of consumption and entertainment- hungry liberal segments avowedly committed not only to breaking the hold of 'corrupt politicians' but also spearheading Pakistani society's quest for what Musharraf, under the backdrop of the so-called 'war on terror', had called 'enlightened moderation'.

Yet, it was not just relatively affluent, urban liberals that coalesced under the PTI umbrella. A more vernacular element of a decidedly more humble background was also mobilised across various developmental geographies. Most significantly, the PTI secured its first victory at the ballot box in war-torn Khyber Pakhtunkhwa (KP) in the 2013 general election. While the party exploded into the spotlight as a viable electoral contender after a mass rally in Lahore in October 2011, it needed time to attract entrenched 'electables' into its ranks to secure a countrywide electoral victory.[6] It did enough to win governmental power in KP province in 2013, discursively mobilising significant numbers of young people around slogans of 'change' in the province's most developed and politically influential region of the Peshawar Valley.

On the surface, the PTI's campaign in KP projected the party as a 'third force' to traditional political elites in a region brutalised by the 'war on terror'. The seeming inability and/or unwillingness of established political parties, including the Pashtun nationalist Awami National Party (ANP), to both break with entrenched logics of patronage and articulate a consistent anti-war position, was crucial in this regard.[7] In fact the PTI's electoral victory in KP was due to the machinations of the state's security apparatus as much as anti-incumbency amongst war-torn populations.[8]

That Imran Khan and his motley crew of supporters were nonetheless able to depict themselves as challengers to the 'elite' speaks to the growing importance of a digitalised field of politics within a youthful demographic easily moved by empty signifiers.

> [T]wo distinct currents of politics underpin the [PTI] – a reliance on traditional dominant classes and their patronage networks to incorporate the urban and rural poor, and the mobilisation of the authoritarian middle class through a discursive politics of anti-corruption. Both currents were, in turn, organizationally and discursively 'sutured' together in the PTI under Khan's populist leadership.[9]

HEGEMONIC FICTIONS, PAST AND PRESENT

The long genealogy of 'anti-corruption' in Pakistan's political lexicon mirrors a parallel fixation with 'development', an idea and material reality with colonial roots. I have already discussed how distinct developmental trajectories have coexisted within

Pakistan's postcolonial social formation, successive hegemonic middle-class moments both cause and consequence of uneven development over time. I now turn momentarily to the global confluence of 'development' with 'terrorism' in the period that was initiated by Washington's announcement of the so-called 'war on terror' in October 2001.

The rise of illiberal 'authoritarian personalities' in western polities in the 2010s reflects underlying contradictions in the liberal-capitalist order traceable at least as far back as the late 1970s. The initiation of the so-called 'war on terror' in 2001 actually triggered the emergence of the far-right and the attendant unravelling of the 'extreme centre'. Arguably the most prominent critical lens through which western statecraft was analysed at the time, particularly following disclosures about the treatment of political prisoners in Guantanamo, was the 'state of exception'.

Giorgio Agamben's book by this name is part of an anthology that interrogates the long history of western sovereignty and law. Agamben draws on traditions of political theory from the interwar years, and the otherwise opposed philosophies of Walter Benjamin and Carl Schmitt most prominently. His treatise concludes: '[T]he state of exception has today reached its maximum worldwide deployment. The normative aspect of law can thus be obliterated and contradicted by a governmental violence that – while ignoring international law externally and producing a permanent state of exception internally – nevertheless still claims to be applying the law'.[10]

In arguing that the 'war on terror' represents the 'maximum worldwide deployment' of a state of exception with a substantial historical footprint, Agamben effectively demolishes claims of liberal statecraft in the western world that extend back to the early modern period. Extrapolating this genealogical argument to Asian and African (post) colonies is even more damning, given how many communities within the historically imperialised zones of the world-system are denied even the pretence of citizenship.[11] Seen thus, the state of exception has been *status quo* in the non-western world since long before the 'war on terror' was initiated.

Furthermore, hegemonic notions of 'rule of law' in the annals of western modernity, however contradicted, have persisted at least in part due to the placation of subordinate classes at home through both organised genocide of indigenous people and the loot of colonised people abroad. This dialectic of passive consent and coercion is as crucial today as it was during the era of direct European colonial rule.[12]

Through the invisibilising of violence and brutalisation to which slaves and their descendants as well as native American populations were subjected, the white settler colony metamorphosed into a polity convinced of its 'manifest destiny'. The mythical 'American dream' of radical individualism and social mobility (for white people) within the polity corresponded to imperial adventures in the name of 'democracy' and 'freedom' beyond its borders.

Alexis de Tocqueville famously penned *Democracy in America* to explicate what he perceived to be a novel social and political form. As a French aristocrat, Tocqueville's myopic personal predilections were anything but democratic.[13] Nevertheless, he presciently warned of tyrannical political potentialities contained within the emergent American polity. As Pence suggests:

> Individualism, which Tocqueville understood as the foreseeable mental outcome of sustained existence under the rough equality of conditions, an ambivalent unity of contradictory longings, describes both a new mode of subjectivity and a new basis for political and bureaucratic control. Individualism for Tocqueville is the emblematic new mode for the production of political subjectivity, insofar as it gives the appearance of offering the materials for successful individuation while simultaneously imposing conformity and homogeneity on each and every subject.[14]

The proverbial tyranny of the majority, then, referred to the prospect of a hegemony sustained by an almost limitless horizon of material advancement for (white) individual citizen-subjects smug in their self-perception as inimitably autonomous beings. Yet this deep ideology has come into increasing contradiction with material reality, and particularly the relative stagnation in standards of living for the largely white middle strata since the 1970s.

This stagnation was glossed over for the most part by the brand of identity politics evocatively captured by the euphemism 'progressive neoliberalism'.[15] In short, the 'American Dream' remained alive and well in the form of selected rags-to-riches life stories of hitherto racialised, gendered, sexualised and other subjects. This ideological fiction was reinforced by the end of the Cold War and attendant triumphalism about the finality of free-market capitalism and its liberal democratic twin.

The historic riches of western capitalist societies, whatever the extent of inequality within them, continue to be sustained by the unevenness of a world-system made through colonial conquest and plunder. Neoliberal globalisation has, nevertheless, coincided with a greater share of wealth and income of global output accruing to the non-western world than ever before. If this has been one of the major contributing factors to the falling star of 'progressive neoliberalism' in western societies, it has been mirrored by an increasingly hegemonic idea of upward mobility in the non-western world not dissimilar to the 'American Dream'.[16]

THE MIDDLE MUDDLE

Processes of individuation in postcolonial societies are not, of course, reducible to the western prototype. But neoliberal globalisation has provided a fillip to a possessive individualism in postcolonial societies often misleadingly analysed through the lens of unchanging kinship ties and other parochial group identifications.

In the introduction, I postulated that the contemporary middle-class moment – and its authoritarian political impulse especially so – has roots in two preceding middle-class moments. The first middle-class moment birthed under colonial tutelage was distinct for its Anglicised character. The proverbial men of letters in occupations such as law, medicine, education and government service claimed to embody the collective will of the fledgling 'nation' whereas they actually represented a privileged section of society.

The second middle-class moment (1977–1999) was precipitated by the deepening of capital in the social formation at large, mechanisation of the agrarian economy and mass migration from rural areas to metropolitan Pakistan and regions like the Gulf. This second moment represented the rise 'from below' of social forces rooted in commerce and manufacturing – the 'intermediate classes' of (post) colonial capitalism. In a nutshell, the middling stratum of society grew in size and scope while its cultural outlook became more variegated, the high moralism of the colonial educated classes eclipsed by a 'democratisation of patronage' and chaotic battles to capture political and economic resources.[17]

The third and contemporary middle-class moment is an historic muddle of social forces. There remains a steady stream of vernacular elements from the 'country' that seek to graduate into the 'town'. Meanwhile, the offspring of the intermediate classes have, over the past several decades, benefited from English education and been exposed to western pop culture via liberalisation and digital media. Then there are the descendants of the colonial men of letters who continue to champion 'middle-class' values, even as they lament the erosion of liberal mores and the colonial public sphere.

As such, neoliberal globalisation has blurred the lines between 'vernacular' and 'Anglicised'. The middle-class aspiration has been imbibed by a large cross-section of society, equating to a far larger demographic than either of the previous two middle-class moments.[18] Any given household can straddle both 'town' and 'country', an older generation unschooled in English and 'bourgeois' ethics, the younger generation fully versed in exactly these ethics.

In practice, contemporary middle-class discourse and political subjectivity is far more diverse than suggested by binaries of political clientelism and 'corruption' on the one hand, and meritocracy and upright personal behaviour on the other hand. 'The middle class, which is institution-specific and cuts across different, often contradictory, ideological divides, has numerous factions as part of it, [none of which] have been a "natural" ally for democrats and have displayed opportunistic (though perhaps, rational) behaviour, compromising at each historical juncture'.[19]

Within the reactionary coalition, affluent class segments propagate rhetoric against the 'other', whether the latter is engaged in banal 'corruption' or is deemed an existential threat to 'national security'. More ominously, less affluent segments aspiring to upward mobility – but often unable to climb the social ladder despite their acceding to the patronage-based rules of the game

– actually embody parochial group identities and become foot soldiers of frequently violent processes of 'othering'.

In the paradigmatic case below, parochial group feelings target certain ethnic groups that remain suspicious in the official (colonised) mind. In the extreme case, the 'other' is rendered a 'terrorist' that must be eliminated. Yet this 'othering', parochial herd behaviour and individuated alienation is just as visible in everyday settings through alarmingly common and gruesome practices like 'honour killings'; targeted violence against religious, ethnic, and sexual communities; or rape and assault against minors, including child labourers.[20]

These forms of othering and violence are not reducible to the logic of capital, and what I have called the middle-class aspiration more generally. But entrenched societal hierarchies and the many forms of violence that are visited upon those who challenge social taboos are in almost all cases conditioned by everyday struggles of working people to navigate the nexus of state and capital.

INSURGENCY-WRACKED INDIA AS 'PAKISTAN'

Everyday forms of injustice and violence in postcolonial society are organic microcosms of the politics of fear championed by the state, propertied classes and patriarchs at multiple higher scales. This historical relationship is epitomised in the current conjuncture by the prosecution of the so-called war on terror. While there is nothing novel about the criminalisation of peripheries in postcolonial countries, the rejuvenation of the state's coercive mandate has been coeval with the 'successes' of high-profile countries like India and China at the zenith of neoliberal globalisation in the late 1990s and early 2000s.

The repetition of the celebratory mantra that openness and liberalisation – 'development' writ large – has lifted hundreds of millions out of poverty, has been the perfect foil for the despoilation of nature and dispossession of indigenous communities and working peoples in centres and peripheries alike. The excesses of Maoism in China, and mediocrities of India's licence Raj have, it has been claimed, given way to freedom – of markets and individuals – not least of all in the case of peripheral subjects brought into the orbit of 'development'.

Dibyesh Anand has argued persuasively that both China and India can be conceptualised as 'postcolonial informal empires', namely large multi-ethnic states which, while laying claim to foundational principles of anti-imperialist struggle, subjugate their own ethnic peripheries. Extractive and punitive logics of Empire are applied by the central state to resource-rich and culturally distinct peripheries, the neoliberal developmental regime thus spawning a 'globalizing bourgeoisie [which] remains subservient to the political privilege of the securitized state'.[21]

The dark underbelly of India's neoliberal developmental regime bears remarkable similarities to Pakistan. For all of the hype surrounding liberalising India – symbolised by euphemisms like 'India Shining' – large parts of India have been wracked by a Maoist guerrilla insurgency, even as decades-old centre–periphery conflicts simmer in Kashmir, Manipur, Assam and Nagaland.

At the start of the millennium, Naxalite rebels laid claim to a swathe of India's territory – the so-called 'Red corridor', stretching from Andhra Pradesh to Bihar – thereby challenging both state and capital. By the end of the decade, then Indian Prime Minister Manmohan Singh decried Naxalism to be a 'menace' and the 'greatest internal security threat to our country'.[22] Today, the Indian state remains locked in a low-intensity war with armed rebels across various terrain, evidence that 'capitalism must always and everywhere fight a battle of annihilation against every historical form of natural economy that it encounters'.[23]

Much like historically 'underdeveloped' peripheries in Pakistan that the state and multinational capital rendered 'productive' from the late 1990s, long-neglected parts of the Indian countryside – particularly those occupied by indigenous populations – were functionally rediscovered along with India's overall rebirth as an 'emerging market'.

Naxalism was initially a movement of landless peasants in West Bengal struggling against 'semi-feudal' classes and the (post) colonial bureaucracy in the late 1960s. By the 2000s, it had established roots in regions like Chattisgarh in which armed conflict raged over rich mineral deposits within densely forested ecosystems. The Maoist struggle against the neoliberal regime, then, was not rooted in the classical peasantry as much as 'tribal' Adivasi populations with distinct cultural norms, historically subjugated by the postcolonial state under exceptional legal regimes. In the current conjuncture, these Adivasis are staving off further relegation to the status of surplus populations.

Ethnographic research on both the Maoist movement as well as the brutalisation of local Adivasi populations by state-backed militias, the Salwa Jundum most notorious amongst them, has elucidated the politics of fear and desire that has played out in Indian town and country alike over the past two decades.[24] I wish to bring into focus how the movement has been constructed as a threat to 'civilised society' and the latter's prized imperative of development. This narrative is illustrated no more strikingly than in the term 'Urban Naxal', which quickly became a one-size-fits-all label with which to demonise dissent of any kind following the election of Narendra Modi's BJP to governmental power in 2014.

Soon after Manmohan Singh declared the Naxal 'terror' as the country's biggest security threat, the Indian novelist Arundhati Roy, having spent time with guerrillas in Chattisgarh, wrote that security personnel and local residents alike used the code 'Pakistan' to refer to Naxalite-controlled areas in conflict-ridden zones. Roy was lambasted in the Indian mainstream for representing the Naxalite cause; within a few years, many other dissident intellectuals, media persons, as well as students were roundly being labelled 'Urban Naxals' espousing an anti-state agenda to be crushed at all costs.

The resort to repressive state nationalism has, I want to reiterate, a long history in India, Pakistan and other postcolonial countries. That a Congress government first invoked the Naxalites as the 'greatest security threat' faced by India is not to be understated.[25] The authoritarian 'turn' in the Indian context represents the intensification of incipient trends rather than a qualitative shift away from a mythical 'democratised' polity.[26]

In a similar vein, the PTI and Imran Khan have consolidated the militarised, financialised and globalised capitalist order to which all regimes after the Musharraf dictatorship also pledged allegiance. The PTI heavily criticised the 'war on terror' in Pakistan during the 2000s and early 2010s, distinguishing itself from 'anti-people' rulers that had forced the country into 'fighting America's wars'. Yet it took the reins of government in Khyber Pakhtunkhwa (KP) province in 2013 when 'counter-terrorist' military expeditions on the Pashtun border with Afghanistan were still ongoing.

The scorched earth operations may have ended by the time Imran Khan was ushered into the Prime Minister's office in 2018, but at the time of writing, the PTI government had done little to arrest the intensifying grip of the military establishment over the economy and polity in general, the ideological prop for which has been the prosecution of unending threats to 'national security' and the country's 'Islamic' ethos.

The Baloch, Pashtun, Sindhi, Siraiki, Gilgit-Baltistani and other ethnic peripheries have always been ruled through unashamedly colonial legal and administrative modalities. Since the onset of the 'war on terror', the footprint of the state's coercive apparatus in these peripheries has in fact grown, even if the military establishment has strategically acceded to nominal changes in the legal-administrative regime.[27] Deeply ingrained notions of the colonised 'other' have been brought to bear amongst captive audiences: fear and desire hegemonised to devastating effect.

During the most intense phase of military operations in the late 2000s and early 2010s, mobilisation of 'public opinion' amongst TV-watching populations in support of 'counter-terrorist' operations in the Baloch and Pashtun peripheries featured two distinct tropes. On the one hand, the hegemonic apparatus appealed to unitary state nationalism, the 'terrorists' seen as conspirators seeking to undermine Islam and Pakistan in cahoots with states as diverse as India, USA, Israel and Afghanistan. On the other hand, everyday racism vis a vis young people migrating into the city from the peripheries illuminated the more molecular underpinnings of contemporary hegemony. Beyond idealised notions of state nationalism, the tenuous desires of racialised, caste-divided and gendered toiling classes for upward mobility into the mythical 'middle class' were mobilised.

THE PROVERBIAL 'OTHER'

As the country's most coherent institutional interest group, symbolised by its self-anointed role as the 'guardian of Pakistan's physical and ideological frontiers', the Pakistani military has over the course of many decades enhanced its multi-faceted project of control over the country's body-politic.[28]

At the outset of the 'war on terror', however, the national security apparatus was beset by contradictions when the military was forced to abruptly renounce its longstanding patronage of Islamist militants and pronounce itself ready and willing to facilitate the US in its prosecution of ex-proteges now turned 'terrorists'.[29]

For decades, official state nationalism glorified '*jihad*' in neighbouring Afghanistan and Indian-occupied Kashmir under the pretext that Pakistan faced a perennial threat from 'enemies' that sought to undermine it. The war on terror, then, forced a messy recalibration of not only strategic goals but state ideology in accordance with an apparent global consensus on 'terrorism'.[30]

The 'war on terror' was experienced in two opposed ways in 'town' and 'country'. The former was a haven for the politics of fear; a captive audience generated to cheer on 'counter-terrorist' operations. The latter was caricatured as a haven of 'terrorists', its complex historical political economy obfuscated accordingly. For the most part, 'terrorist strongholds' were allegedly concentrated in KP province, and the adjacent Federally Administered Tribal Areas (FATA) on the northwestern border with Afghanistan, from where attacks on civilians in Pakistani towns and cities were said to be launched.[31]

In the initial phase of the war on terror, the state's official policy featured 'peace deals' with certain militant factions characterised as 'pro-Pakistan'. By 2007, however, with the military increasingly under fire for protecting rather than eliminating 'terrorists' – and thus facing suspension of US military aid – the dominant *modus operandi* became scorched earth military incursions to eliminate 'terrorist strongholds'.[32] I will return later to the dynamic anti-war movement by the name of the Pashtun Tahaffuz Movement (PTM), which articulated the suffering and emancipatory ideals of brutalised Pashtun youth before, during and after these military operations. For the time being, I draw attention to how the signifier of 'terrorism' ignited the politics of fear in metropolitan centres.

The first mediatised counter-terrorist operation was undertaken in the Swat Valley at the northernmost reaches of KP province in 2009.[33] Swat is a popular tourist destination for both down-country Pakistanis as well as foreigners, popularly described as the 'Switzerland of Pakistan' for its snow-capped peaks and manicured skiing destinations. Notably, it was also the case study of a series of seminal anthropological investigations of the class and status configuration of agrarian 'Pashtun society' between the late 1950s and 1980s.

By 2009, Swat bore little resemblance to the society chronicled in earlier scholarship. The region had been considerably transformed by out-migration, the expanding role of commercial classes, and the emergence of the religious right as a major player in local politics. I have elsewhere undertaken an historical-sociological analysis of millenarian politics in Swat, showing how motifs of divine salvation and immediate material mobility generated a following for religious militancy in the region.[34]

Local dynamics and state machinations aside, the sensational narrative that militants were '160 km from Islamabad' engendered panic within the Pakistani mainstream. The tipping point was the release of a video in which militants in Swat were seen flogging a young girl, precipitating a frenzy within liberal circles about the existential threat to 'civilised' and 'law-abiding' residents of the federal capital.[35]

The alarmism that gripped Pakistani liberals in 2009 was reminiscent of the lead up to the US invasion of Afghanistan when the imperative of 'saving Afghan women' from the Taliban built on a more generalised narrative that 'terrorists' were targeting the American 'way of life'.[36]

The Swat operation 'successfully' cleared the Valley of 'terrorists', ostensibly averting the impending spread of 'extremism'. The politics of fear, however, would continue to be generated in subsequent years, with more operations taking place in Waziristan, Bajaur, Khyber and other tribal districts. On each occasion, systematic propaganda campaigns coordinated by the Pakistani military's Inter-Services Public Relations (ISPR) served the purpose of generating a visible gallery of vociferous support.[37]

The spillover effects of countless operations in Pashtun peripheries buttressed the politics of fear in a more molecular fashion. In 2009–2010 alone, an estimated 3 million residents of the Swat Valley were forced to flee their homes, languishing in makeshift camps in neighbouring districts or finding their way to urban centres like

Islamabad, Lahore and Karachi to take refuge with different family relations.[38] Already burgeoning ethnic tensions in megacities like Karachi were thus ignited, particularly under the city government of the Muttahida Qaumi Movement (MQM), a prominent ally of the Musharraf regime and major player in Karachi's rapidly changing political economy landscape since the 1980s.

As Pakistan's major manufacturing centre at the highpoint of the state's tryst with import substitution industrialisation, Karachi was, until the late 1970s, the hub of a vibrant organised labour movement in which up-country migrant workers coalesced around leftist ideologies of class in ways that appear unthinkable in the current conjuncture. From the 1980s onwards, however, working people from Punjabi, Urdu-speaking, Sindhi, Baloch, Pashtun, Siraiki and other ethnic backgrounds became increasingly confined to insular neighbourhoods. Left-progressive political ideologies and formations were displaced by reactionary forces as ethnic identity was politicised in increasingly violent ways. Under the regime of neoliberal globalisation, ethnic divisions hardened further, particularly as land became a coveted financial asset over which vertically organised ethnicised political factions attempted to wrest control.[39]

Pashtuns from toiling backgrounds in metropolitan areas – both long-term residents as well as those forced to flee their war-torn homes in the northwest – found themselves in the crosshairs of violence and discrimination, with some retrogressive Muhajir and Sindhi nationalist elements previously at loggerheads coalescing around the imperative of countering 'Talibanisation' of the metropolis, implying that all Pashtuns were 'terrorists' threatening the city's civility. Ethnic profiling in major urban centres intensified with each passing operation, even as evidence confirmed that the majority of victims of 'terrorist' violence in Karachi as well as cities and towns of Punjab were 'Pashtuns, religious minorities, and people belonging to the lower-middle class'.[40]

PLANET OF SLUMS

Crucially, 'development' in the city proceeded apace, with already ghettoised ethnically and religiously insular working communities being subjected to summary evictions to make way for commercial plazas, as well as gated housing communities.[41] One such massive demolition drive took place in the federal capital of Islamabad in July 2015, a scene in which I was a principal protagonist as a political organiser working with the residents of a Pashtun *katchi abadi* (squatter settlement).[42]

Situated on the outskirts of the city adjacent to the fruit and vegetable wholesale *mandi* (market), the settlement in sector I-11 of Islamabad was given the name 'Afghan Basti' by the municipal authorities, indicating both how Pakistani Pashtuns can be conveniently identified as 'outsiders' and referencing the historical origins of the settlement which came into being in the mid-1980s when the anti-Soviet *jihad* in Afghanistan forced many Pashtuns living along the western border to flee into Pakistani cities.

The *katchi abadi* had grown exponentially due to another wave of migrants in the wake of military operations during the war on terror, a younger generation of family members from the border districts taking shelter with the earlier generation that had originally built the settlement. Islamabad, like other major metropolitan centres in the country, is increasingly a living embodiment of what Mike Davis iconically name the Planet of Slums:

> [F]ormal housing markets across the 'Third World' rarely supply more than 20 per cent of new housing stock, so out of necessity, people turn to self-build shanties, informal rentals … or the sidewalks. Illegal or informal land markets have provided the land sites for most additions to the housing stock in most cities of the South over the last 30 to 40 years.[43]

In this parallel housing market too, networks of patronage are inscribed upon circuits of capital featuring middlemen, state functionaries, landlords, and the proverbial wretched of the earth.[44]

By 2015, the city's authorities and real estate dealers saw the I-11 squatter settlement as 'wasted' real estate. A public relations campaign was thus launched that employed standard signifiers: 'development' was being held back by unruly elements, at best illegal encroachers and at worst potential 'terrorists' with links to those holed up in the remote Pashtun tribal belt, perhaps even the proverbial 'foreign hand'.

The television and newspaper media faithfully propagated the official narrative. Following months of resistance by political organisers and residents alike, a 'grand operation' levelled the settlement leaving 25,000 Pashtun men, women and children homeless.[45] Copious use of force was followed up by a police case under Anti-Terrorist legislation.[46] Even after homes were bulldozed to the ground and dozens incarcerated, the environment of fear was sustained with police officials making public announcements in surrounding areas warning local residents not to take in any of the evictees, let alone rent property to them. Many residents within surrounding neighbourhoods were in any case glad to be rid of the squatters, having lamented that the latter were responsible for depressing land values in the neighbourhood.[47]

Such modalities of the formal state and the subjectivities of even those of relatively humble origins seeking to at least maintain and at best enhance their social standing encapsulate the dialectic of fear and desire. By supporting violence against racialised working communities, the aspiring middle-class subject not only demonstrates loyalty to the state but also enhances the prospective values of one's own assets. In this brittle and increasingly atomised existence, commodity fetishism and hate are presented as the only tickets to something resembling a dignified life.

THE DAILY TEXTURE OF NEOLIBERAL HEGEMONY

The question is whether the majority of the toiling millions who aspire to be 'middle class' can realise their dream and come to reside in what I have figuratively called 'town'. Positing this question is to reemphasise two related aspects of hegemony that speak both to how Gramsci originally conceptualised it and the specificities of the current conjuncture.

First, aspirations to 'middle-class' life are not founded upon false consciousness, if that means a genuinely believed falsehood. What Gramsci calls the 'fact of hegemony' is 'ethico-political' and also 'economic'; it is a worldview, a mode of self-conduct that both conditions and is conditioned by irreducible material terrain upon which everyday life is lived. In the context of postcolonial capitalism, this material terrain is ruthless: class combines with ethnicity, gender, religion and caste to make life a daily battle to navigate state and market. For many, survival demands acceding to the rules of the game without climbing the social ladder *per se*.

Second, contemporary hegemony is extremely volatile. The notion that anyone can 'make it' certainly appeals to the instinct of smartphone-wielding young people in an increasingly mediatised and commodified social universe. But the 'breakthroughs' of mythical rags-to-riches persona who possess no previous sources of wealth are exceptional, and not untypically drenched in cynical rivers of blood and dispossession.

Nevertheless, middle-class aspiration remains hegemonic due to the absence of an alternative worldview in which cooperation rather than competition for resources and opportunities structures not only political life, but the very basic choices being made by the youthful majority about livelihoods and other basic material needs.

I now offer a brief sketch of the daily texture of neoliberal hegemony for the youthful middle-class subject in our digitalised present.[48] There are few studies about the subjectivities of young Pakistanis who become involved in 'novel' kinds of work driven by online platforms, even though anecdotal evidence suggests that Pakistan is home to one of the fastest-growing populations of young people engaged in such forms of work. The Global Gig Economy Index of 2019, for instance, claimed that the number of digital 'freelancers' in Pakistan increased by 42% between 2018 and 2019, describing 'Pakistani youth [as] fuelling the gig-economy explosion'.[49]

Notions such as 'self-employment', 'flexibility' and 'easy money' conveniently gloss over the fact that much of the workforce in postcolonial societies like Pakistan is in any case 'informalised'. Most labour arrangements, including self-employment, prop up what are at best precarious livelihoods, and at worst forms of indentured/unpaid labour. In fact, purportedly immaterial labour is intricately tied to supply chains in which acute exploitation of workers and natural resources represents the largest single source of profit.[50]

Silvia Federici minces no words about this obfuscation: 'I do not accept the concepts of "cognitive capitalism" and "immaterial labour", which ... privilege a particular sect of workers as the revolutionary subjects. It is a Eurocentric concept, which forgets what it takes to produce computers and other forms of digital technology'.[51]

Nevertheless, the hegemonic appeal of the commodity form, actualised through advertising, projects the 'gig economy' to a burgeoning population of young people in lieu of permanent and secure employment. Take the example of the rush of young men (and to a lesser extent women) that responded to the launch of the ride-sharing application Careem in 2017 by buying new cars on lease and becoming Careem 'Captains' across metropolitan centres in Pakistan. As in most countries, decades-old taxicar and rickshaw industries were totally transformed virtually overnight.[52]

An average Careem 'contractor' could make a down payment of as little as Rs. 200,000 for a budget, locally manufactured Japanese model car, with monthly instalments of between Rs. 10,000-12,000. Spending 8–10 hours on the road, convincing their passengers to give them good reviews post-ride, and the monthly bonuses that followed, could generate, at least in an early honeymoon period, a monthly income of up to Rs. 60,000. Within 18–24 months, the investment made on the vehicle would be recovered, and the middle-class aspirant could consider purchasing another vehicle to put out for hire.

Early birds experiencing initial 'success' subsequently found their incomes drying up as more Careem Captains entered the labour market. Vehicles became increasingly costly to maintain, given the wear and tear of constant use. To maintain consistent levels of income, then, meant working longer hours, and supplementing driving with other work in the gig economy – inevitably precarious as well.[53]

Economic slowdown during the pandemic affected Careem Captains acutely. But the fact of a saturated labour market was apparent long before the pandemic, the glitz and glamour of 'flexibility' and 'autonomy' quickly displaced by insecurity and uncertainty. The Careem Captain is a microcosm only of the mythologised digital 'freelancer' more generally, a mediatised representation that manipulates material reality as much as reflects it.[54]

THE GENDERED MIDDLE-CLASS SUBJECT

The journalistic and academic mainstream loves 'women's empowerment'. Alongside education, arguably the most powerful trope in the contemporary language of 'international development' is that of expanding female participation in the labour force. The argument is that bringing more women into the realm of paid work – whether by extending opportunities for home-based workers or by facilitating mobility into public spaces – correlates with greater decision-making power for women within otherwise extremely stifling patriarchal households, and, for that matter, wider community settings.

I noted in the introduction how Bangladesh was one of the 'success' stories of the neoliberal developmental regime; the highly feminised garment industry is not only said to have contributed to export-led growth but also enhanced women's mobility, decision-making power, and educational prospects for subsequent generations of girl-children.

Nuanced and critical scholarship has deconstructed many of these claims, noting at one and the same time the centrality of paid work for the upward mobility and autonomy of young working-class women, while also clarifying just how exploitative and hazardous it is.[55]

That the aspirations of young working women (many of whom carry multiple burdens of housework, care and waged employment) are limited to 'empowerment' as it is conceptualised in the hegemonic mainstream is not hard to understand – the logic of capital demands it. Young Pakistani women and girls working as domestic servants, in sectors like cigarette-rolling and bangles, and as agricultural labourers enjoy little 'empowerment'; many endure sexual and other forms of violence to earn a pittance of their male counterparts.[56]

Further up the class ladder, the tech-savvy Pakistani woman aspiring to middle-class status covets employment – or even 'entrepreneurial' – opportunities in online start-ups.[57] Such opportunities no doubt constitute a push back against decades of obscurantist social norms in one of the world's most male-dominated public spheres. For instance, women Careem Captains and bike riders are now spotted on Pakistani roads where even a decade ago they were conspicuously absent.[58]

Yet, the political horizon represented by such individuated subjectivity is best captured by the term 'corporate feminism'. If reduced to a 'handmaiden of capitalism', feminism is little more than a rallying cry for 'the benefits of exploitation in the workplace and oppression in the social order [to be] equally shared between ruling-class men and women – a form of 'equal-opportunity domination'.[59]

Most young Pakistani women hardly see themselves as charting a path for any kind of feminism at all – I will return to the polarisations expressed through and in Pakistan's contemporary feminist movement in the next chapter. But 'corporate feminism' – or liberal feminism broadly conceived – retains hegemonic pretensions in large part because it often does not need to name itself at all. Insofar as a greater percentage of young women and girls increasingly connected to the 'global village' become willing and able to defy entrenched patriarchal norms to join the labour market to enhance their standards of living, they in effect reinforce middle-class hegemony.

There is no predetermined limit on young women's political agency. I have argued throughout this book that the sheer demographic weight of young people in regions like South Asia and Sub Saharan Africa, alongside the volatility of the contemporary rule of capital, suggest contingent possibilities over the medium and long run that may not necessarily be palpable in our crisis-ridden present. In any case, whether or not the middle-class subject recognises the limits of liberal feminism will be conditioned by how critically and self-reflexively she engages in an increasingly digitalised field of politics. It is to this most vexed of questions that I turn next.

3
The digital lifeworld

> All fixed, fast-frozen relations, with their train of ancient and venerable prejudices and opinions, are swept away, all new-formed ones become antiquated before they can ossify. All that is solid melts into air, all that is holy is profaned …
>
> Marx and Engels, The Communist Manifesto

In 2016, at the annual summit of the global ruling class known as the World Economic Forum (WEF), Chief Executive Klaus Schwab announced that humanity is now firmly in the throes of the 'Fourth Industrial Revolution'. Building upon 'the digital revolution that has been occurring since the middle of the last century', The Fourth Industrial Revolution 'is characterised by a fusion of technologies that is blurring the lines between the physical, digital, and biological spheres'.[1]

Read as a utopian imaginary, Schwab's words evoke modernity's final frontier, a social world in which the human intellect completely tames nature, transcends all its hitherto known physical limits, and heralds a fantastic era of peace and prosperity. In practice, digitalisation offers no respite from our crisis-ridden present, actually reinforcing the relations of force that undergird an increasingly volatile and destructive capitalist social order.

Nevertheless, digital utopianism remains prominent in the contemporary mainstream, exemplified by celebrity tycoons like Elon Musk masquerading as great innovators. This techno-optimism persists at least in part because of its gradual yet unmistakable convergence, in metropolitan western societies at least, with counter-cultural currents associated with the New Left of the 1960s and 1970s.[2]

The digitalisation of social life in postcolonial countries like Pakistan has proceeded along a distinct trajectory to the prototypical 'network society' in the Euro-American heartlands of the world-system. The speed with which digital technologies, smart gadgets and social media platforms have taken root in and are transforming non-western societies is unprecedented. Grafted upon entrenched class and other forms of social polarisation, the so-called 'digital divide' is also of far greater magnitude in post-colonial South Asia and Sub Saharan Africa than anywhere in the world.[3]

Despite the unevenness with which technological developments are impacting the historical peripheries of the world-system, however, the hegemonic narrative of hundreds of millions – if not billions – of Asians and Africans being extricated from poverty into the fabled 'middle class' is both enabled and embodied by an increasingly digitalised lifeworld.

The state and big business in 'emerging markets' champion both investments in digital technology and the imperative of incorporating hitherto excluded subjects into digital networks.[4] Construction of fibre-optic cables and mobile towers is accompanied by the marketing of budget smartphones and mobile internet, while the imperatives of 'financial inclusion' are now fulfilled through modalities such as mobile banking.[5] As I noted at the end of the previous chapter, the expansion of circuits of capital and the creation of consuming subjects that facilitate the realisation of profit are grafted onto normative ideals such as 'empowerment'.[6]

Put differently, digital technology is now of central significance in the universalisation of the commodity form, and, more specifically for the purposes of my argument, middle-class aspiration. In this chapter, I delve further into the manner in which digital networks are increasingly conditioning Pakistan's political sphere. Along with the TV media, social media has rapidly emerged as the most significant terrain for the dominant hegemonic apparatus to propagate the dialectic of fear and desire, generally in concert with established terrain such as the home, school, workplace and place of religious worship. At the same time, the field of politics is becoming increasingly complex, the digital space sometimes obscuring and even challenging established networks of political patronage.

This is most evident in the countervailing online voices that contest state, class, patriarchal, ethnic-national and other entrenched structures of power. Digitalised resistance to excesses of power does, in some cases, buttress political collectivities on the ground. On the whole, however, unmediated online 'voice' and the espousal of maximal political positions against the military establishment, propertied classes and patriarchal power more generally, has not halted the juggernaut of fear and desire. The highly politicised digital space breeds its own forms of parochialism that hinder the construction of what Gramsci would term a national-popular will.

Even on platforms boasting greater participation of classed, caste-ised, gendered and racialised subjects, the logic of capital remains, for now, largely uncontested. Meanwhile, the burgeoning surveillance capacities of the contemporary state are steadily consolidated with the wilful collaboration of Big Tech.

OF MANY PUBLICS

Structural transformations through time and space have produced new middle-class subjects while transforming the hegemonic apparatus itself. In Gramsci's words, a hegemonic apparatus in any particular conjuncture 'creates a new ideological terrain, determines a reform of consciousness and of methods of knowledge'. In no uncertain terms, the digitalised field of politics represents a new ideological terrain that is transforming consciousness – of self and the social world at large – through novel methods of knowledge.[7]

I have argued that contemporary middle-class hegemony has been preceded by two distinct moments in Pakistan's history that have also been hegemonised through a middle-class political subject. All three moments have corresponded to both an idealised as well as a practical manifestation of the 'public', within which, in turn, all historically specific forms of 'the political' have taken form. In a nutshell, neither the 'public' nor 'the political' is static; in fact, as I will discuss presently, the quest for hegemony is a struggle between multiple 'publics' as much as competing conceptions and political practices.

My point of departure is Nancy Fraser's seminal critique of the Habermasian ideal-type 'public sphere' in which nominally 'equal' citizens engage in voluntary deliberation and thereby buttress processes of democratisation.[8] Actually existing western society, Fraser asserts, has been historically constituted through sexist, racist, class and other structures that continue to shape social relations, and, therefore, access to the public sphere. She proposes the alternative normative ideal of multiple publics so as to ensure a meaningful voice for the 'unequals' that comprise contemporary capitalist society.

Read as a general critique, Fraser's argument can ostensibly account for any number of societal contexts. Yet, the specificity of the (post) colonial public sphere demands interrogation in its own right. Habermas' conceptualisation of the public sphere was, after all, based exclusively on Europe's distinct experience of bourgeois modernity. Kaviraj notes that 'in Indian society there was a rich repertoire of concepts of common responsibility, obligation, action, that did not share the characteristic features of bourgeois publicity like a recognisable source, proper authorization, impersonality, legality, state sanction, and clear ascription of individual responsibility'.[9]

The colonial interregnum, then, brought into existence distinct norms and practices of publicity that had little organic basis within Indian society *per se*, instead imposing 'from above' officially-mandated norms that corresponded to the dictates of state and capital. Pride of place in the officially constituted public sphere was of course accorded to the men of letters that were 'Indians in blood but English in taste', at least some of whom, it is worth reiterating, hailed from big landed families.

This explicitly insular domain corresponded to sanitised forms of 'the political'; less than 12% of the total population was entitled to vote in provincial elections held in colonial Punjab under the 1935 Government of India Act.[10] Eventually, the contradictions of colonial statecraft and its associated legal instrumentalities – rooted in a hybrid property rights regime in which capital accumulation was interwoven with the geopolitical imperatives of Empire – exploded the 'official' public sphere from within. Both a burgeoning nationalist element and other 'publics' espoused unruly political forms challenging state, capital, and entrenched patriarchs more generally.

Seminal theorisations of 'the political' in (post)colonial settings have grappled with what has generally been perceived as a bifurcated public sphere; the subaltern studies school originally postulated the simple conceptual binary of 'elite' and 'subaltern', one of its most prominent members more recently deploying a parallel binary of 'civil society' and 'political society'.[11]

Tracing 'the political' through time and space demands a dialectical, or, a la Gramsci, boundary-traversing approach – simple binaries cannot quite capture the complexity, I think, of what are multiple publics that intertwine and overlap, along with political ideas and practices.[12] The need for dialectical approaches to make sense of multiple publics and corresponding political forms has become more pronounced in an increasingly digitalised lifeworld.

Insofar as the politics of fear and desire is emblematic of a volatile structure of power, the left's inability to step into the proverbial breach is a conspicuous aspect of the current conjuncture. In the remainder of this book, I will turn specifically to modalities of left praxis in the present, and consider if and how a viable and mass politics of the left can be imagined and constructed in our time.

It is certainly necessary, as per one of Marx's famous dictums, to engage in ruthless criticism of everything regarding the revolutionary imaginaries, organisational methods, and claims to representation of the left in the 20th century. At the same time, one of the major draws of the revolutionary left in the previous century was that it possessed a futuristic horizon of systemic change across unevenly developed geographies and social differences.

Notwithstanding the manner in which online spaces facilitate exposure to political ideas and forms on a global scale, the reflexive theorisation of an increasingly digitalised field of politics and the middle-class political subjects that exercise agency therein is an urgent task that has yet to be attended to in postcolonial countries like Pakistan. In the absence of a thoroughly historicised theory of contemporary – and particularly digitalised – political forms, the dialectic of fear and desire will continue to prop up the dominant hegemonic apparatus. Inadvertently or otherwise, progressives will aid and abet state and capital in the reproduction of antagonistic difference instead of fomenting an alternative hegemony and attendant political forms.

THE NEW SUBJECTIVITIES

In the four decades since the intensely reactionary and imperialist-backed military regime of General Zia ul Haq banished revolutionary imaginaries to the margins of society, innumerable Pakistani 'publics' have emerged bearing the imprint of many different political subjects beyond the stylised progressive vanguards of the 20th century – the anti-imperialist intelligentsia, the industrial proletariat, and the peasantry.

Politics 'from below' in many postcolonial settings has been theorised extensively, the particularism of emergent political subjectivities, and everyday strategies to navigate state and market amongst prominent themes of this scholarship. These theorisations, I want to emphasise, take certain normative horizons as given. As Aronowitz explains in a classic essay penned at the dawn of neoliberal globalisation: 'Political life is no longer rooted in a conception of a qualitatively better world. Even social movements, which in the 1970s accused the political parties, left and right, of operating without vision, have ceased articulating their utopias and sunk into Realpolitik'.[13] Moreover, while politics during the heyday of revolutionary internationalism was collectivist in both identity and organisation, political forms since the end of the Cold War have been described as decidedly more individualist, featuring 'less class, more irreverence'.[14]

When these trends are refracted through our digitalised present, a number of contradictory trajectories can be identified. First, we see the proliferation of many digital publics in which political identities and positions are shaped and articulated. These publics include but are not limited to oppressed genders, castes, religious communities and peripheral ethnic nations. In a very short period of time, these digital publics have become the most significant gathering 'places' of young political subjects that resist state power, patriarchal violence, racial/ethnic privilege and so on. A related feature of these digital publics is a trenchant critique of intellectual vanguardism as well as exhortations about the adequate representation of historically underrepresented genders, castes and ethnic nations.[15]

Second, an even bigger segment of youth come together in lower-class publics, which facilitate various forms of socialisation and avenues for entertainment.[16] Interactive video games like PUBG as well as the Chinese application Tik Tok have millions of Pakistani users, which dwarf explicitly political publics like Twitter. Such digital publics suggest definitively that, even for those lower down the social ladder, 'pleasure is at the forefront of digital life'.[17] Seen thus, the mass of people euphemistically called the 'global poor' do transgress cultural and class norms as *individuals* who conceive of themselves as *users* of technology. But these transgressions rarely translate into anything like collective challenges to gender, caste and state-nationalist ideology, let alone a hegemonic left politics.

The emergence of innumerable digital publics and the opportunities for agency provided therein for millions, if not billions, of young South Asians and Africans is certainly not to be understated. That a greater segment of society than ever before are able to participate in digital publics represents some sort of advance from the classed, gendered, racialised and caste-ised blinkers of public spheres and political forms of the past.[18] Yet, the innumerable youthful subjects articulating their 'voice' in online spaces tend to aggregate into little more than 'digital swarms' that come together only fleetingly around 'fits of outrage'.[19] It can even be argued that 'revenge capitalism' has goaded the left into a *cul-de-sac* of 'revenge politics'.[20]

Exposed to diverse ideas and collectivities through online spaces, most young people able and desiring to be incorporated into the digital lifeworld imbibe a dominant neoliberal subjectivity. We must come to see prevailing online etiquettes as *individuating* people – creating the feeling of atomisation without autonomy – who are in turn *used by corporations* to generate profit. Meanwhile, complex political, economic and cultural structures – both within the nation-state boundaries and at the regional/global scales – remain underspecified.

It is worth being reminded that the PTI generated much rhetoric about challenging 'elite dominance' while deploying idioms of 'revolution' and 'change'. As in other parts of the world, such rhetoric has not undermined complex structures of power in Pakistan. The rejection of 'elites' is conflated with contempt for politics at large; it is thus that the PTI and other such contemporary ideological and political formations lay claim to being 'apolitical' and/or incorruptible.

Juxtaposed upon this is the fact that most young people in Pakistan participate in the digital lifeworld as commodity-consumers; their politics, then, at best conforms to what is known globally as 'woke' culture. The whims of 'wokeness' are exemplified most in the manner that protagonists can become part of 'troll armies' to drown out oppositional voices. Critical scholarship on contemporary politics in western countries during and after the experience with demagogues like Trump has demonstrated how social media platforms like Twitter contribute to hateful herd behaviour to incredible effect.[21]

In Pakistan, the PTI is not alone is in mobilising 'troll armies' from amongst youthful populations. Other parties like the PML-N and PPP who have constituted the 'extreme centre' for most of the neoliberal interregnum also dedicate considerable energy and resources to retrogressive online mobilisations. Then there is the religious right, which widely deploys digital technology to expand its support base.

Over the past 4–5 decades, religio-political organisations have carved out institutional spaces that accord them captive audiences and pockets of popular support. Parties like the Jama'at-e-Islami (JI) and Jamiat-e-Ulema-e-Islam (JUI) have established electoral constituencies on the basis of entrenched networks of patronage. Many religio-political organisations also benefit from a massive infrastructure of religious schools (*madrassahs*) where young people can be groomed ideologically and mobilised for political ends.

During the so-called 'war on terror', the liberal mainstream's primary focus has remained on the role of the prototypical *madrassah* student. But it is not only young *madrassah* students who are drawn to right-wing militant ideologies and mobilisations. As such, religiously infused educational curricula, mainstream media narratives and a broad consensus within the political mainstream have all contributed to the post-1980s consolidation of what I have called 'Zia's generation'.[22] Under the 'war on terror' regime, a large segment of this generation has become convinced that 'Islam' is under attack from both imperialist powers and puppet rulers within Muslim countries.

Digital spaces have contributed greatly to the emergence of new religio-political movements that both deploy established political idioms, while shaping new forms of militancy. The reconquest of Afghanistan by the Taliban in August 2021 after 20 years of American occupation triggered a wave of 'celebration' amongst

Taliban supporters within Pakistan – many of the younger generation of sympathisers conducting well-organised campaigns in digital spaces to propagate notions of a 'reformed Taliban 2.0'.

Meanwhile, the Tehrik-e-Labbaik-Pakistan (TLP), which came into being as late as 2016, has, in a few short years, generated eye-catching online support around 'blasphemy' related causes.[23] Highly disciplined social media teams are regularly able to trend hashtags that dwarf others. TLP founder Khadim Rizvi, who died in early 2021, acquired almost cult-like status due to viral YouTube videos of his fiery speeches. Significantly, the TLP has also repeatedly succeeded in staging prolonged street mobilisations that other political forces struggle to match.

While there is little doubt that Deobandi, Wahhabi and more recently Barelvi militancy in the form of the TLP has benefited from patronage by the military establishment, many religio-political movements have nevertheless evolved an organic support base. Only two years after its founding, the TLP secured tens of thousands of votes within the developed Punjabi heartland in the 2018 general election. In effect, the TLP appeals to less affluent segments with which mainstream parties have instrumental links. In any case, all of these political forces resort to the politics of fear and hate to appeal to a demographic characterised by unmet aspirations for upward mobility.

Social media platforms that reinforce simple binaries of 'us' and 'them', provide a fillip exactly to such a xenophobic politics. It is a matter of conjecture whether a wider cross-section of people either not yet using social media or less willing to commit to supporting such causes is actually supportive of exclusionary religious symbols, mobilisation or violence *per se*. It is arguably this proverbial 'silent majority' that can and will shape the struggle for digitalised hegemony in years to come.

ECONOMIES OF REPUTATION

Notable exceptions aside, progressives occupy echo chambers in which outrage *vis a vis* an oppressive 'other' is often given voice through maximal positions.[24] More often than not, this tendency culminates in a 'competition of oppressions'; feminists 'call out' Marxists for their relative inattentiveness to the imperative of adequate representation of women and gender minorities; Pashtun, Baloch and other ethnic-nationalists decry the lack of concern of feminists to the plight of war-torn peripheries; and, the left more broadly is criticised for its 'class reductionism' by both nationalists and feminists.

This bickering reflects 'the politics of recognition in the age of social media'. Largely subservient to the business model of platform capitalism, our individual subjectivities produce 'economies of reputation'. Rivalry and inequality are persistent: '[E]ach participant arrives with a different quantity of reputational capital and is immediately confronted by the dominance of those with more'. Competition, rather than cooperation, is the default *modus operandi*. In the final analysis, 'people who are both economically privileged and culturally included can end up feeling like they are neither of those things'.[25]

Particularistic identities can certainly be dialectically enjoined to what Fanon called 'universalising values', and on the surface at least digital publics would seem to be ideal conveyor belts for such values because they can connect progressives from across the globe. When uprisings like the so-called Arab Spring and Occupy Wall Street became lightning rods for tech-savvy youth around the world, digital networking was identified as central to the initial success of these mobilisations.[26]

Yet embryonic coalitions that came together across many social divides subsequently fragmented. The subsequent reassertion of militarised class, gendered and other structures of power in highly repressed and inegalitarian societies like Egypt suggests that even if digitalised resistance can generate occasional victories against reactionary forces, it does not in and of itself precipitate the construction of a viable historical bloc to challenge the logic of capital and the militarised postcolonial state.[27]

Left-progressives in the current conjuncture face a challenge to hegemonise their struggle not unlike that which confronted their 20th-century predecessors. Then too, many revolutionaries struggling against the state, class and imperialist structures of power hailed from 'middle-class' backgrounds. The imperative of devising an alternative hegemony made those middle-class subjects the vectors of revolutionary internationalism across distinct social formations and geographies.

The imaginaries championed by the classical left were, ultimately, unable to transcend the logic of capital, colonial statecraft and patriarchy. It is now a matter of historical record that this failure is explained at least in part by the fact that majoritarian ethnic and religious groups, high castes and men were overrepresented within the left intelligentsia.

The greater diversity in composition and horizons of left-progressives in the current conjuncture suggests that the failings of previous generations have been named and lessons learned. But what of self-reflexivity with regard to contemporary left praxis? Is there a political horizon beyond the pitched battles to preserve or enhance reputations on social media platforms? What of hegemonic imaginaries of 'development' that animate the contemporary crises of capitalism, the plight of the most exploited classes and the destruction of nature? Youthful middle-class political subjects active in digital spaces who espouse progressive positions must, quite simply, develop a common agenda for the future. Dean asks and answers rhetorical questions in this regard:

> Are online practices of sharing and opining, Twitter storms and Facebook updates, the practices of a political subject? What about hacking or blogging? Perhaps most important, do we proceed as if this subject were individual, or collective; is it present in the actions and events carried out in its name and, if so, how? Communicative capitalism supplies the infrastructure for this spontaneous politics of the individual: mobile phones and social media. What passes for politics enslaves individuals ideologically to bourgeois individualism and its individualised political practices.[28]

Absent universalist principles, what Dean calls the 'spontaneous politics of the individual' in an increasingly digitalised lifeworld, cannot save, let alone displace, crisis-ridden structures of power. The predicament of mass representation under conditions of neoliberal capitalism is intensifying *despite* the growth of burgeoning digital publics comprised of politicised young people. Insofar as the latter subscribe – consciously or otherwise – to a hegemonic middle-class aspiration, the emancipation of the wretched of the earth and rehabilitation of nature will remain a footnote in the often frenzied 'online practices of sharing and opining'.

DIGITALISED RESISTANCE

The Pakistani case converges with many other postcolonial contexts in which youthful populations drawn into the hegemonic web of middle-class aspiration buy into motifs of militaristic or religiously infused nationalism that reinforces antagonistic difference. Counterposing desire and fear is a successful strategic peg for reactionary forces that forge cross-sectional coalitions including historically oppressed castes, genders and ethnic nations: where the promise of upward mobility from 'country' into 'town' falters, blame is apportioned to the proverbial 'other'.

Modi and the BJP in India have instigated 'widespread attacks on Muslims' in which 'large numbers of Dalits, Tribals and women [have taken] part'.[29] Meanwhile, disaffected lineages of industrial labour that has historically supported social democracy in the US, UK and other western countries have supported Trumpism, Brexit and other far-right coalitions.[30]

Disaffected social classes and oppressed segments have also mobilised along progressive lines, and I document here two popular struggles in Pakistan that have brought into focus regimes of dispossession, imperialist war and patriarchy. Most prominent is the youth-led movement against the state's prosecution of the 'war on terror' in the tribal Pashtun districts that erupted into the Pakistani mainstream in 2018. The Pashtun Tahaffuz Movement (PTM) exposed not only the quite tenuous dialectic of fear and desire and the attendant town-country divide, but also the increasing centrality of digital networks in the struggle for hegemony.

Recall that the PTI has been able to generate a following in the relatively developed Peshawar Valley of KP province, the historic heartland of Pashtun nationalism, where the famed Khudai Khidmadgar movement led by the Ghaffar Khan, also known as the 'Frontier Gandhi', took root. A movement rooted in the grievances of middle peasants against the large landed families enfranchised by the colonial state, the Khudai Khidmadgars eventually metamorphosed into the National Awami Party, a mass party of the anti-imperialist left in which all of Pakistan's oppressed ethnic nations were also represented.

With the decline of the left from the late 1970s onwards, NAP ceased to be a multinational formation with a clear socialist bent. A burgeoning Pashtun commercial segment based in and around Peshawar became the moving force of the party, in turn mobilising trading interests in Pashtun-majority areas of Balochistan province, the port city of Karachi as well as small towns and cities across Pakistan.

Rechristened as the Awami National Party (ANP), the party has subsequently been engaged in uneasy tussles for governmental power, resources and identity with Pakistan's militarised establishment, its leaders and rank-and-file periodically subject to state repression. Crucially, Pashtuns have been inducted into civil and military services in growing numbers over time, and today are second only to the Punjabi ethnic majority in terms of representation within the state.

As the heartland of classical Pashtun nationalism *and* home to the most educated and aspiring Pashtun youth, the Peshawar Valley symbolises a unique dialectic of resistance and accommodation, the 'war on terror' bringing both historical and contemporary contradictions to the fore. In successive elections since 2002, the Valley has voted in a six-party coalition of the religious right: Muttahida Majlis-e-Amal (MMA); the ANP; and finally, the PTI. With anti-incumbency, war-weariness, and the growing influence of tech-savvy youth on political discourse all at play, a young population that came of age under the shadow of war – but still heavily integrated with mainstream Pakistan – ultimately put its lot in with the PTI's heavily choreographed politics of 'change'.

Development was one of the PTI's important sells for this youthful demographic, gated housing schemes, shopping malls, roads and a highly publicised albeit stop-start Bus Rapid Transit (BRT) scheme serving an increasingly urbanised Peshawar Valley. The majority of the Valley's youthful aspirants to middle-class status have yet to graduate into the proverbial 'town'. Even so, the PTI has continued to rely on motifs of 'anti-corruption' and 'development', its power buttressed by the patronage of the military establishment.[31]

The party boasts a highly weaponised online support base, which came to the fore most spectacularly following the emergence of the PTM. While the latter has claimed to speak for all Pashtuns, its genesis lies in the suffering of war-ravaged populations in the considerably less economically and politically integrated tribal districts bordering Afghanistan. A significant segment of Pashtun youth from the Peshawar Valley have opposed the PTM, their middle-class aspirations trumping a potentially collective transformative politics against war, militarisation, and disenfranchisement.

In its earliest incarnation, the PTM was the Mehsud Tahaffuz Movement (MTM), a largely online advocacy platform established in 2014 by a handful of students of Gomal University in Dera Ismail Khan. The MTM sought to draw attention to the devastation caused by land mines in the tribal district of Waziristan planted during the spate of military expeditions since 9/11, and the plight of hundreds of amputees hailing from the Mehsud tribe in particular.[32]

The MTM generated a non-negligible following but was unable to generate a critical mass of support that could puncture the establishment's 'counter-terrorism' echo chamber. The January 2018 killing of Naquibullah Mehsud by police in Karachi, a young native of Waziristan who had migrated to the metropolis to find employment, dignity and peace, however, triggered an uprising unprecedented in Pakistan's recent history.

With the original MTM organisers in the lead, a young man named Manzoor Ahmed most prominent amongst them, a protest march from Dera Ismail Khan to the capital Islamabad culminated in a *dharna* (sit-in) which soon metamorphosed into what became known as the PTM. Within a few days, incessant Pashto-language chants of *Da Sanga Azadi Da?* (What kind of freedom is this?) were ringing out amongst thousands of protestors at the *dharna*, many of whom were migrant workers and students in Islamabad and its twin city of Rawalpindi. Thousands more tuned in to live streams broadcast by the young protestors themselves, armed only with a smartphone and 3G internet connection.

The *dharna* forced into the public spotlight not only Naquibullah's encounter killing but the plethora of flagrant abuses of power by security personnel in the prosecution of the 'war on terror' in Waziristan, neighbouring districts and indeed, amongst vulnerable populations – Pashtun and otherwise – across Pakistan. Manzoor Ahmed, a child of war only 8 years old when the 'war on terror' began, took on the *nom de guerre* Manzoor Pashteen, symbolically embodying leadership of the proverbial Pashtun nation. Able to articulate his people's sufferings in extremely intimate ways, Pashteen also demonstrated great analytical nous, clearly and bravely naming the local, national and global classes and institutions that prop up both Pakistan's national security state and the imperialist 'war on terror'.

Pashteen and the PTM took on the mantle of Badshah Khan and the *Khudai Khidmatgars* to dazzling effect, decrying a Great Game with long historical genealogies and coming to exert a moral authority amongst a critical mass of Pashtuns in the tribal districts craving peace and liberation from the nexus of Taliban, American/NATO troops, and Pakistan's security establishment. Perhaps more significantly, Pashteen's appeal extended to a broader cross-section of progressives.

During and after the Islamabad dharna, Pashteen's online persona went viral. Through live Facebook streams, Pashteen reached millions, most of them young, including in an increasingly restive Punjabi heartland. PTM's core constituency, its rank-and-file, was Pashtun youth who spread Pashteen's message in the mould of citizen-journalists who propagated information and organised public events through social media platforms.

The ANP, led by Ghaffar Khan's grandson Asfandyar Wali Khan, inadvertently provided a swathe of younger members to the PTM, who saw in the emergent movement a willingness and ability to speak truth to the state's coercive apparatus in ways that the ANP – along with most of Pakistan's bourgeois parties – refused to do. In effect, the ANP and other established ethnic-nationalist parties were left in the wake of a reinvigorated Pashtun nationalism which literally created its own cadre as thousands of previously inactive youth were politicised and made the digital into a powerful space of dissent.

Invited to meet with the army leadership, Manzoor Pashteen's demands were acknowledged and promises made to stop the humiliation of FATA residents at security checkpoints, de-mining of the tribal districts, recovery of those who disappeared during military operations, and finally arrest of the police officer who fired the shots that killed Naquibullah Mehsud.[33]

But as the PTM ripple effect intensified – and especially following mass mobilisations in Pakistan's two biggest cities of Karachi and Lahore in which Pashtun youth came together with Punjabi, Sindhi and other progressives and the prospect of a wider anti-establishment peace movement emerged – the army's posture shifted markedly. Mainstream politicians and the TV media soon wanted to have nothing to do with the PTM. Narratives of foreign conspiracies replaced the earlier empathy for the movement's leaders.

The only means remaining for PTM to propagate its demands was social media. While many progressives online did rally around the PTM, an organised assortment of hyper-nationalist trolls – often operating numerous 'fake accounts' doing the bidding of the military's Inter-Services Public Relations (ISPR) wing – reasserted hegemonic state nationalism with full force.[34] Young Pashtuns ostensibly 'loyal to Pakistan' were mobilised to delegitimise the PTM and cast aspersions on the means and methods of its leadership.

The mobilisation of tribal factions in Waziristan against PTM's relatively inexperienced and youthful leadership, harkening to modalities of indirect rule from the British period, was one tactic. A legion of abuse was also instigated in online spaces. Cosmopolitan and relatively affluent Pashtun media personalities, including young women exposed to western education, proclaimed loudly that Pashtuns were equal Pakistanis.[35] Confident and assertive women leaders of the PTM were pilloried relentlessly through misogynistic and threatening content – one eventually fleeing Pakistan and settling abroad.[36]

The ISPR has in fact invested heavily in digital media of all kinds through the 'war on terror' conjuncture. It funds the making of songs and films imparting nationalistic content, often coinciding with major military expeditions and war commemorations.[37] Even more noteworthy is the active recruitment of young people to the digitalised hegemonic apparatus. Regular internships are offered for both young men and women, representing both an opportunity to develop personal contacts within the military institution and to acquire the skill set necessary for long-term engagement within the media industry.[38]

A recently published manuscript on the mobilisation of affect to serve the state's militarist project highlights 'the use of militarised imagery in popular culture; militarisation of university and research agendas; making of national histories to glorify military action; and belief that military efficiency is integral to state survival and security'.[39] While historical social networks remain important cogs in the militarist wheel, the digitalised hegemonic apparatus, peopled by 'loyal' political subjects with their own middle-class aspirations, is rapidly attaining primacy.

Even so, PTM has exposed chinks in the ruling bloc's armour. It confirms the fragility of militarised hegemony and has sent shockwaves through the national security apparatus. At the time of writing, PTM retains a substantial online following, and digitalised resistance has largely corresponded to consistently large offline mobilisations. For all of its successes, however, the PTM is, ultimately, an ethnic-national movement with diverse ideological inclinations. These differences became clear in September 2021 when one of the movement's main leaders announced the formation of a separate political party largely comprised of new and old Pashtun nationalists.[40]

Not dissimilar limitations inhibit another relatively successful contemporary movement enabled by online mobilisation, which has been described as embodying the 'fourth wave' of Pakistani feminism.[41] Led by young, digitally connected women and girls, this movement is symbolised by an annual countrywide mobilisation on 8 March (International Women's Day), which spontaneously began in 2018 under the guise of 'Aurat March'. These mobilisations, and the demographic of mostly young women that spearheads them, has forced a feminist narrative without precedent into the extremely insular and patriarchal Pakistani mainstream.

Despite being one of the world's most male-dominated societies, characterised by extremely high and acute levels of sexual violence, as well as extremely gendered public spaces, Pakistan has never boasted a broad-based feminist movement. For the most part, 'women's rights' advocates have been socially liberal and well-educated urbanites. One interlocutor has accordingly argued that '[i]n the Pakistani context it seems more appropriate to speak of a women's movement which has some feminist underpinnings'.[42]

While some of the impetus provided to this movement during the Cold War came from the organised left, the latter was itself male-dominated and generally at pains to overcome its basis in the colonial educated classes. It certainly did not accord primacy to patriarchy in its historical materialist reading of Pakistani state and society.

With the emergence of the digital lifeworld, tech-savvy young women and girls have erupted into the public eye. If a female middle-class subject has been at the forefront of movements like the Aurat March, women and girls from less affluent backgrounds, whose mobility is policed to a far greater extent, have also been enabled by digital publics. Many populate digital spaces from within the confines of what in Pakistan is commonly called *chadar* and *chardiwari* ('the veil' and 'the walled home').

It is within such restrictive and conservative social environments that the epidemic of violence against women, including so-called 'honour killings', is most pronounced. Young women that transgress established norms and exercise individual autonomy in their choice of marriage – or the bigger taboo of extra-marital relations – are often served a customary punishment of death. Sexual violence and other forms of patriarchal control are also exercised over women and girls in more urbane, 'bourgeois' settings.

The 'fourth wave' of Pakistani feminism, then, specifically challenges 'control over the female body and sexuality, on which rests the entire edifice of patriarchy'.[43] The Aurat March in fact acquired immense public visibility because of one of its initial slogans. *Mera Jism Meri Marzi* (My body, my choice) elicited a wave of reaction which united not only the religious right but significant segments of mainstream political parties, and the intelligentsia at large. Perhaps most notably, it triggered waves of online hate, abuse and harassment against Aurat March organisers.

By 2020, after two successive years of intense vitriol, at least some Aurat March chapters began to diversify their agenda and articulate positions related to ethnic-national, class and other forms of privilege, while also naming the militarised state apparatus as the repository of Pakistani patriarchy. Perhaps unsurprisingly, tensions within the otherwise fluid composition of Aurat March reared their head. Organisers explicitly wanting to project a universalist politics – or a 'feminism for the 99%' – proceeded to distinguish themselves by adding the appellation 'Azadi' (freedom) to the original Aurat March name.

The more expansive ideological outlook of the Aurat Azadi March meant lesser visibility for slogans like *Mera Jism Meri Marzi* and greater emphasis on dispossession, war and other manifestations of neoliberal capitalism. Control over the female body at the level of the private patriarchal household was thus linked to a broader structural critique of state and capital, sexual violence connected to systemic reproduction of racialised, classed, caste-ised and religious differences.

This more nuanced critique has to date not been accompanied by significant offline mobilisations of working women and other oppressed segments. This confirms the limitations of Aurat Azadi March organisers who still rely, with notable exceptions, on digital publics largely peopled by middle-class political subjects. Whether or not organic linkages develop with the proverbial wretched of the earth in times to come remains an open question. Acknowledgement of the often chaotic and reactionary etiquettes of online activism would be the first step.

Even lacking the substantial mobilisation of subordinate class segments, the Aurat Azadi March's increasingly radical positions have certainly rattled Pakistan's military establishment, its organic intellectuals as well as patriarchs young and old across the social formation. In 2021, the Islamabad chapter of the Aurat Azadi March was explicitly targeted by a serious of trumped-up blasphemy allegations clearly designed to silence that segment of the organisers seeking to cultivate universalist sensibilities.[44] The attacks were based on the manipulation of online content, illuminating again the increasingly ruthless struggle for hegemony in the digitalised political field.

That repression has been employed against movements like PTM and AAM makes clear that the militarised state apparatus and dominant social forces more generally recognise their hegemonic potentialities. Bannerji notes that 'feminist anti-racist social movements … [are] intrinsic to building new conceptions of class and class politics'.[45] So long as the contingent possibilities of a universal, emancipatory political horizon remain open, the gains of digitalised resistance can, through appropriate strategic means, be hegemonised.

WHAT IS TO BE DONE?

Digital spaces mediate the gap between hegemonic middle-class aspirations and actually existing material terrain. Social media provides avenues for dissent but also coercion and consent-generation. One progressive scholar argues: 'From within digital capitalism, socialists have found a way to use social media platforms to produce, circulate, and consume abundant socialist media and cultural expressions in opposition to capitalism'.[46] But capital profits from their activities all the same.

If young people in western societies 'are using platforms to reclaim and remake the word "socialism" into something cool, attractive, reasonable, and viable to more and more people', there is, as yet, no comparable achievement to boast of in the postcolonial regions of South Asia and Sub-Saharan Africa. There certainly may be in the future, but this will happen only if important objective constraints and dominant subjectivities are acknowledged and strategies shaped accordingly.

To the extent that the 'digital divide' is being bridged in countries like Pakistan, it will help Big Tech, namely Google, Amazon, Facebook, Apple and Microsoft (GAFAM), 'enlarge its already gigantic global footprint'.[47] Chinese social media platforms like TikTok have enjoyed exponential growth in a short period but, as yet, cannot compete with the scale and scope of GAFAM.[48]

In the western heartlands of the world-system, awareness about the significant and increasing power of Big Tech is significant and growing. The latter's collaboration with the contemporary state has provided a major fillip to surveillance technologies; it is thus that the imperative of protecting 'privacy' has become a major tenet of liberal politics.

More generally, the COVID-19 pandemic has also brought into sharp focus the 'Amazonisation of everything'.[49] Apple and Amazon generated unprecedented profits during lockdowns even while large segments of humanity, including many capitalist firms, suffered unprecedented losses. The proliferation of critical scholarship centring concepts such as data colonialism, even if somewhat rudimentary, speaks to growing awareness about novel forms of commodification of social life.[50]

In Pakistan and other postcolonial contexts, Big Tech is not generally conceptualised as part of the dominant structure of power. Selective activism is prevalent in progressive circles whereby social media platforms like Facebook and Twitter are lobbied to regulate hate speech and/or push back against Pakistani state repression in digital spaces. But as I have already noted repeatedly, the 'progressive' moniker in Pakistan does not equate to an explicitly 'socialist' or 'left' politics. Liberal positions, in fact, enjoy greater purchase in online spaces. Critiques of the state, patriarchy and ethnic-national oppression thus often remain isolated from a wider interrogation of capitalistic logics, including those of Big Tech.

Demands for extension of communications infrastructure and digital technology to under-serviced regions, girls/women and 'the poor', will not necessarily deepen radical critique and generate revolutionary sensibilities. I am certainly not suggesting that left-progressives distance themselves from such demands.[51] But subjective interventions above and beyond infrastructural and digital outreach are the sufficient condition to generate universalist imaginaries and practices of politics that transcend the logic of capital.

The digital lifeworld is not yet all-encompassing, and limiting ourselves to consideration only of the subjectivities generated within it effectively reinforces contemporary hegemony. I turn now to a barebones universalist political theory that centres but also seeks to displace the hegemonic middle-class subject.

4
The classless subject

> To transform the external world, the general system of relations, is to potentiate oneself and to develop oneself ... the synthesis of the elements constituting individuality is 'individual', but it cannot be realised and developed without an activity directed outward, modifying external relations both with nature and, in varying degrees, with other men ... For this reason one can say that man is essentially 'political' since it is through the activity of transforming and consciously directing other men that man realises his 'humanity', his 'human nature'.
>
> Gramsci, SPN 360; Q10II§48

At the conclusion of his magisterial account of the short 20th century (1914–1991), the revolutionary imaginaries embodied by socialist states, national liberation movements and insurrectionary ideologies like Marxism at their nadir, Eric Hobsbawm wrote: 'The world of the third millennium will almost certainly continue to be one of violent politics and violent political changes. The only thing uncertain about them is where they will lead'.[1]

The regime of neoliberal globalisation was inaugurated at the end of what Hobsbawm called the 'age of extremes' to unprecedented fanfare, proclamations of peace and prosperity ostensibly consigning 'violent politics' to the proverbial dustbin of history. The neoliberal fantasy has unravelled spectacularly in the intervening three decades, intensifying ecological, economic, political and cultural crises. Wars, dispossession and banal violence in new and old peripheries alike have intensified. Understood as a totality, the global political economy is in the throes of an endless crisis, the most apparent manifestation of which is the rule of hate-mongering megalomaniacs.[2]

In at least some parts of our putatively shared world, the Euro-American heartlands of the global capitalist order most notably, the crisis of 'the political' would appear to have clearly decipherable roots. Following Gillian Hart, I have argued that contemporary right-wing authoritarianism is best understood within a global conjunctural frame; the present book is a modest attempt to place the historic peripheries of the world-system front and centre within exactly such a frame.

In doing so, I have sought to bring into focus crucial particularisms of the postcolonial condition. Such particularisms also apply to left praxis. While the experiences of the contemporary left in the western heartlands of the world-system can be instructive, theorising emancipatory politics in non-western postcolonial countries must correspond to grounded material realities.

What has become known as 'millennial socialism' in western societies has given rise to the parallel political tendencies of Corbynism and Bernie Bro's in the UK and the US, respectively, as well as experiments like Syriza (Greece) and Podemos (Spain).[3] The failure of all of these formations to become hegemonic alternatives despite ongoing eruptions of popular discontent – take, for example, the resurgence of the Black Lives Matter (BLM) movement in 2020 – can be explained by a number of related factors.

First, 'millennial socialism' has not, to date, been able to win the support of a cross-section of older generations in ageing societies and, relatedly, significant segments of (white) working people. Second, the institutional logics of electoral democracy have been hollowed out through the neoliberal interregnum, and are now virtually hostage to corporate money and power, as well as geopolitical imperatives upheld by states across the globe. Third, the historic social democratic parties in western countries contain a significant 'extreme centre' that opposes its own more radical currents tooth and nail.[4]

Yet even if the contemporary left in western societies remains wedded to 'folk politics' that militates against the construction of an alternate hegemony, movements like Occupy were successful in 'transforming the public discourse around inequality'.[5] This is to say that 'millennial socialists' are anything but a fringe current in society, despite being a minority demographic in an otherwise ageing population.

In contrast, Pakistan has one of the most youthful populations in the world, with 35% of its approximately 230 million people below the age of 14, and 65% below the age of 30. The rest of South Asia and Sub-Saharan Africa have similar demographic profiles. Most millennials in these regions have limited exposure to socialist ideas; in Pakistan, this youthful mass largely ascribes to demeaning caricatures of the left weaponised by the state and reactionary forces.

Popular struggles like PTM and Aurat March have politicised youthful populations but still fall short of mobilising a critical mass beyond particular constituencies. Other progressive forces call attention to the relentless excesses of the neoliberal developmental regime, most notably myriad forms of dispossession that brutalise working masses in both metropolitan areas and remote peripheries while damaging already fragile ecosystems. But the hegemonic dialectic of fear and desire remains entrenched, tropes of 'development' and 'terrorism' ever-present in digital spaces as well as historical consent-generating terrains of home, school, workplace, mosque and the corporate media.

As such, therefore, resistance – in its current online and offline forms – is *necessary but not sufficient* for widespread social transformation. Progressives involved in almost perpetual firefighting against innumerable excesses of power are, in fact, unable to extend their temporal frames beyond the present, and thus make little headway in theorising and formulating strategies to redress the endless crisis. In this chapter, I offer some tentative ideas about the forging of a national-popular will to actualise a hegemonic alternative. I euphemistically and provocatively name this political horizon and the collectivity that embodies it the 'classless subject'.

No political organisation in Pakistan today embodies a national-popular will, let alone a revolutionary imaginary that can be hegemonised across unevenly developed geographies. Once-upon-a-time social democratic parties like the ANP and PPP certainly claim to be the vanguard of democracy, leading the challenge against a predominantly Punjabi military establishment, as well as the militant right-wing. Baloch, Sindhi, and other ethnic-nationalist parties on the fringes of the political mainstream make not dissimilar claims. But none of these self-professed 'progressive' forces commands a critical mass of support within the developed Punjabi heartland. As I suggest presently, it is within this context that a meaningful emancipatory politics must be fomented, the classless subject at the vanguard.

REVOLUTIONARY IMAGINARIES, PAST AND PRESENT

> A struggle which mobilizes all classes of the people and which expresses their aims and their impatience, which is not afraid to count almost exclusively on the people's support, will of necessity triumph.
>
> Frantz Fanon[6]

In the introductory chapter, I briefly touched on the vexed and highly polemical debates that have often posited class and identity at two poles of an irreconcilable spectrum of critical theory. I noted that postcolonial theory has for the most part been suspicious and even dismissive of universalist political projects, and attendant political subjectivities. By way of a brief historical excursus, I make the case that dialectical conceptualisations of class and identity, and the particular and the universal, constitute the hegemonic terrain for an emancipatory politics in postcolonial contexts.

The 'new social movements' which emerged in western society during the 1960s and 1970s were both cause and consequence of postmodernist disillusionment with the rational subject of liberal and even Marxian folklore. These movements announced the organic emergence of multifarious political subjects espousing many different autonomous notions of freedom. Overturning patriarchal and racial domination, sexual liberation and ecological restoration were amongst the various ends to which these different political subjects aspired. Class came to be perceived as only *one* potential expression of political identity, with the (male) proletarian subject relegated from its previously unchallenged status as a revolutionary vanguard.

In short, recognition became at least as important as redistribution. Shifts in the global political economy from the Fordist ideal-type towards flexible forms of accumulation were coeval with the change in tone and tenor of politics.[7] With the collapse of actually existing socialism, the politics of recognition became increasingly individualised and thereby more easily co-opted by the discursive and material logics of the 'free market'. In the previous chapter, I noted, following Davies, that social media platforms are engendering mutation of the politics of recognition into competitive 'economies of reputation'. In such a milieu, to call for a politics, as Nancy Fraser famously did, that combines the imperatives of recognition and redistribution is all well and good, but requires far more elaboration, particularly in a context as far removed from the western prototype as Pakistan.[8]

The argument that I have presented through the course of this book has emphasised the centrality to contemporary hegemony of a middle-class political subject in the postcolonial regions of South Asia and Sub-Saharan Africa. While middle-class hegemonies have undergirded repressive regimes in previous conjunctures too, today's middle-class subject has a far more diverse gender, ethnic and religious background than its predecessors. It is able to articulate itself in and through many 'publics' that digitalisation has brought into being. Finally, it is exceedingly young, and will therefore shape political debate and practice for decades to come.

In a sense, then, this political subject carries within it the seeds of universality – it has the potential to articulate demands for recognition of diverse identity groups, and the demographic weight to embody the aspirations for material uplift of a broad cross-section of society. The prospects of the hegemonic middle-class subject adopting a conception beyond fear and desire – given the 'economies of reputation' that pervade the digitalised field of politics – depend on the renewal of a particular-universal dialectic of redistribution and recognition with historical precedent.

Contemporary middle-class political subjectivity, as I have defined it, features a desire for upward mobility. There are certainly self-anointed 'middle-class' segments that already enjoy high-status positions in society, the descendants of the colonial (wo)men of letters most notable amongst them. But the middle-class subject that is both cause and consequence of the regime of neoliberal globalisation remains largely in the process of becoming, its aspirations typically loftier than what it is actually able to achieve.

Notwithstanding the volatility of 'middle-class' status, the hegemonic apparatus propagates an almost limitless 'desire named development'.[9] The challenge for left-progressives, I think, is to conceive of an imaginary of development that acknowledges the material needs of the mass of (young) working people who seek a 'better life', while at the same time refuting capital's logic of dispossession and brutalisation of the wretched of the earth, alongside despoilation of nature.

Around the world, Pakistan included, the left has struggled to conceptualise a horizon beyond the uncritical embrace of Progressivism and Industrialism that was symptomatic of actually existing socialism in the 20th century. At the risk of oversimplification, those attempts to construct a post-capitalist society were somewhat successful in meeting basic material needs for a wide cross-section of society, albeit at considerable cost for excluded minoritarian groups. Alongside the social and environmental fallouts of the rapid development of productive forces, state socialist projects championed an imaginary of human personhood that denied difference and dissent, and therefore failed singularly in addressing questions of individual freedom and recognition.

Long before most state socialist projects met their end, Gramsci was alive to the dialectic of self, cognitive activity and collective political struggle:

> One could say that each of us changes himself and modifies the complex relations of which he is the hub. In this sense the real philosopher is, and cannot be other than, the politician, the active man who modifies the environment, understanding by environment the ensemble of relations which each of us enters to take part in. If one's own individuality is the ensemble of these relations, to create one's personality means to acquire consciousness of them and to modify one's own personality means to modify the ensemble of these relations.[10]

Gramsci's was not alone in calling for a self-conscious revolutionary political subject that pushed back against teleological assumptions of *Progress* seamlessly ushering in a classless society. Among others, Che Guevara famously wrote that 'to build communism it is necessary, simultaneous with the new material foundations, to build the new man and woman'.[11] Marx's brief reflections on the 'realm of freedom' beyond the 'realm of necessity', featuring an 'association of free producers', also clarified that revolutionary politics is nothing less than a conscious and dialectical transformation of self and community.[12] Most relevant to the postcolonial condition were Fanon's seminal – albeit gendered – formulations about a 'new man' beyond the caricature offered by 'Europe'.

Along these lines, I ask: can the contemporary postcolonial 'middle-class' subject rehabilitate the revolutionary humanism that for some decades in the mid-20th century was a genuinely hegemonic horizon of freedom for all peoples? Insofar as desire for the benefits of development extend to large segments of contemporary humanity in Pakistan and the rest of the postcolonial world, the answer to this rhetorical question demands attention be paid to 'the ethical aspects of such desire if one is to plumb the depths of the human predicament today'.[13]

Contemporary political and social struggles like those that I mentioned in the previous chapter contain embryonic 'ethical aspects'. PTM, for instance, articulates a desire for an end to war and suffering, and the redressal of logics of uneven development that have blighted the Pashtun periphery for decades, centuries even. Mallick offers an eloquent articulation of PTM's potentialities in extending its 'partisan-universal' horizon to a 'concrete-universal' that speaks to other ethnic-national groups and toiling classes at large.[14]

Meanwhile, the Aurat Azadi March, which in its genesis is not a political movement that speaks for subaltern women and an alternative developmental paradigm *per se*, nevertheless posits a politics of recognition in some dialogue with a politics of redistribution.[15] The emergence of a youthful feminist political subject in contemporary Pakistan in any case represents a step towards 'class struggle [that] revolutionises commonplace, everyday ways of living and common sense, as well as social production and reproduction'.[16]

Many decades ago, during the conjuncture of decolonisation – even as the 'national bourgeoisie' was betraying the cause of national liberation – Fanon retained hope in the 'small number of honest intellectuals, who have no very precise ideas about politics, but who instinctively distrust the race for positions and pensions which is symptomatic of the early days of independence'.[17]

Today's putatively 'honest intellectuals' are those young political subjects for whom the ideological props of state, capital and patriarchy have been demystified and the attendant 'race for positions and pensions' displaced. I have repeatedly asserted that a radically expanded 'public' in the context of digitalisation has in any case transformed the very meaning of 'intellectual'. Gramsci's famous adage, of course, challenged the binary of intellectual and non-intellectual *tout court*: '[A]lthough one can speak of intellectuals, one cannot speak of non-intellectuals, because non-intellectuals do not exist'.[18]

Gramsci's insight is, in our times, extendable to its contingent limits. Hence 'honest intellectuals who have no very precise ideas about politics' can, in fact, constitute a veritable hegemonic mass. Indeed, I would argue that this potential hegemonic mass can draw upon the foundational idea of politics, however 'imprecise', that motivated native intellectuals in the period before and after formal independence from colonialism.

This idea was, simply, that all human beings, and colonial subjects especially so, are deserving of the freedoms that the all-knowing coloniser insisted for centuries were his alone. That the promises of modernity – of freedom from material want, hereditary status, and all other forms of oppression – can, in fact, be realised by non-white peoples of the world too. 'The anticolonial desire to modernize' Chakrabarty notes, 'was not simply a repetition of the European modernizer's gesture'.[19]

The hegemonic middle-class subject shaped under the regime of neoliberal globalisation is imbued with a desire that is dialectically born and nurtured alongside fear. Commodity fetishism rules, and insofar as there is a conscious selfhood that is both cause and consequence of this desire, it is covetous and increasingly atomised.

'Anticolonial desire', in contrast, represents a different subjective horizon altogether. It certainly contains the seeds of individual aspiration – for freedoms of all kinds – but these are dialectically connected to the social body as a whole, the political community constituted in and through the liberation struggle. Prior to neoliberal counter-revolution, the political horizon of revolutionary internationalism expressed through this 'anticolonial desire' was conceptualised as 'worldmaking' in and through a 'new man'.

Let me quote Fanon at length to make my point clearer:

> Humanity is waiting for something other from us than … an imitation, which would be almost an obscene caricature …

> [I]f we want humanity to advance a step further, if we want to bring it up to a different level than that which Europe has shown it, then we must invent and we must make discoveries... For Europe, for ourselves and for humanity, comrades, we must turn over a new leaf, we must work out new concepts, and try to set afoot a new man.[20]

This is both a call to transcend capitalist modernity, and to shape the revolutionary subject that is both creator and embodiment of the future society. To be recognised as fully human and accorded the dignity denied by colonialism was as significant a component of the freedom struggle as fomenting a model of development to meet material needs, dismantle class privilege, and reconfigure global political economy alongside.

The intellectual who led this struggle was ultimately not up to the task. Recall that Fanon lamented not only the 'intellectual laziness' of the 'native middle class' but also his 'spiritual penury'. The failure to live up to the 'ethical aspects' of the anticolonial desire for modernity is, today, less significant than the awareness that such ethical aspects existed at all. The challenge of our times is for 'honest intellectuals' to translate and uphold this revolutionary horizon.

It is under this backdrop that I deploy the signifier of the 'classless subject'. On the one hand, this is an assertion of political intention against the hegemonic apparatus that kicked into overdrive at the end of the Cold War, projecting a neoliberal utopia in which class as a subjective category was evicted from the intellectual and political mainstream alongside imaginaries of revolutionary internationalism. A parallel movement took place in the academic realm: Grand narratives, and Marxism in particular, were depicted as reductionist, unable to account, at the very least, for the politics of recognition.

Emphasis on difference and the politics of recognition has, as I have noted repeatedly, been coeval with conspicuous silence about the hegemonic middle-class aspiration. In its other meaning, then, the term 'classless subject' harkens to a rehabilitated 'communist horizon', a universalist project that envisions a world beyond exploitation and oppression. Such a revolutionary imaginary acknowledges the real history of capital and its (re)production of difference – and thus the particularisms of subject positions – but nevertheless posits a universal subject of emancipation.

Climate change, widespread militarisation and financialisation, and the inequity, injustice and oppression that follow, force the very middle-class subject produced, but yet ultimately alienated by the contemporary hegemonic order, to confront what Rosa Luxemburg deemed the choice between socialism and barbarism. The classless subject can meet her material needs without relinquishing individual and collective freedoms. She can struggle for a rehabilitated relationship between humanity and nature, while acknowledging and even encouraging human difference.

It goes without saying that such a political horizon is far removed from actually existing postcolonial society. Middle-class hegemony in the current conjuncture refracts more brutalising forms of colonial statecraft and capital accumulation than ever before, not to mention everyday violence at molecular scales.

To rehabilitate anticolonial revolutionary humanism, then, at the very least entails re-educating contemporary political subjects about the otherwise subsumed radical histories of the immediate post-independence period. Excavating 'utopian and revolutionary pasts' is 'an invitation to alternate ethical subjectivities and possibilities that seem increasingly foreclosed in contemporary South Asia today'.[21]

For organisers of contemporary progressive movements – or what Denning, adapting Gramsci, calls 'legislators' – this re-education can also inform greater self-reflexivity, thereby facilitating translation of yesterday's revolutionary horizon into our times so as to fashion a 'collective organism [that] embodies an achieved unity'.[22] The challenge, as ever, is to identify the various social forces that can forge this collective organism in the wake of neoliberalism's ongoing implosion.

Class

I have not undertaken a comprehensive mapping of Pakistan's class structure in this book *per se*. From their subject positions as primary protagonists of revolution in the 20th century, 'workers' and 'peasants' have been relegated to the margins of the political and intellectual life. Extending these categories beyond the ideal-type – of industrial proletariat and small/landless farmer – will clarify that they are not only still salient but central to a theory and practice of emancipatory politics in our times.

I noted in the introduction that the classical capital–wage labour dialectic does not capture the complexity of postcolonial capitalism: official statistics suggest that less than 40% of the formal labour force is engaged in waged employment.[23] The biggest concentration of waged workers is found in agro-industrial sectors like textiles where subcontracting and sweatshop-like working conditions are the norm. Child labour is common in brick kilns, football stitching and carpet-weaving, while women workers dominate seasonal labour markets in agriculture, domestic service, and specialised sectors like cigarette (*bidi*) rolling and bangles.

It goes without saying that organising such workers – who toil amidst great precarity and in fragmented spaces – is extremely difficult.[24] There are certainly successful examples of mobilisations under conditions of 'informality' in Pakistan and beyond.[25] But these mobilisations are, by definition, difficult to extend to the rest of the 'working class', broadly conceived. They certainly have not been able to halt the juggernaut of right-wing authoritarianism.

What remains of a 'labour movement' in Pakistan – less than 3% of the total workforce is unionised – is limited to an increasingly toothless public sector. Workers in the commanding heights like Railways, Water and Power and Telecommunications have historically enjoyed permanent employment, housing and guarantee of pensions after retirement. Struggles against privatisation led by public sector trade unions have mostly been unsuccessful, most notably that of the Pakistan Telecommunications Limited (PTCL) in 2005.[26] More generally, 'pocket unionism' has become rife, a labour aristocracy and a demobilised workforce together combining to enshrine economism, cynicism, and the politics of patronage.[27]

Most working people remain outside of the imagination, let alone mobilisation efforts, of an already emaciated workers movement. Certain self-employed segments have attempted to unionise over the past 2–3 decades, including rickshaw and taxi drivers as well as street vendors. The former have had whatever little bargaining power they enjoyed decimated by the

Careem-Uber 'revolution', while street vendors' efforts have been overdetermined by middlemen with links to officialdom.

I should also note here that increasingly prominent instances of 'digitalised resistance' are typically divorced from the 'conventional' forms of class struggle spearheaded by the organised trade union sector. The latter's conceptualisation of 'class struggle' is shaped by its very specific and increasingly exceptional objective working environment. Struggles for housing and other basic amenities not directly linked to the point of commodity production are rarely considered part of the trade union mandate. Meanwhile, the middle-class subject leading 'digitalised resistance', I have already noted, is generally disconnected from 'offline' struggles, especially those espousing class as the unifying political identity.

More generally, the contemporary middle-class subject is increasingly drawn to livelihood opportunities through start-ups, paid social media content and e-commerce. As part of a teeming 'white-collar' workforce, s/he is largely motivated by a desire to graduate into what I have called the proverbial 'town'. In a similar vein, most of the 'intermediate classes' which were the motor force of post-Green Revolution urbanisation, spearheading small and medium enterprises in transport, construction, logistics and retail, among other sectors, hailed from classical 'working-class' backgrounds, and/or 'peasant households'. For more than a generation, organised class politics has been the exception, upward mobility via prevailing patronage networks the rule.

This brings me to the 'peasantry'. While processes of de-peasantisation have a longer history, the peasantry has so far appeared in my post-Cold War narrative as the largest segment of the 'surplus populations', having been forced out of its historical abodes in geographical peripheries as well as rural and peri-urban Punjab. For the most part, erstwhile 'peasants' seek out livelihoods in metropolitan Pakistan, although migrating abroad remains a coveted option.[28] As such then, the classical producer-consumer 'peasant household' can only now be apprehended inasmuch as it is problematised.

At the very least, it is important to bear in mind that the category of 'small and landless peasantry' – insofar as this refers to farmers with direct control over agricultural land operating at or close to margins – is increasingly less coherent as contractual and seasonal labour arrangements proliferate. More and more small owner-operators are leasing out their land to those with greater holdings of capital, the former unable to keep up with ever-increasing prices of agricultural inputs and indebtedness more generally.[29]

A radical research agenda on the agrarian question has to consider interlocking agro-ecological crises, and the prospects of various forms of peasant political agency.[30] My only contribution in this regard is to posit regimes of dispossession as constituting the objective universe within which subjectivation of small and landless farmers and other segments of the rural poor takes place.[31] Prospects of organised politics, while not exhausted by the objective realities of dispossession, follow accordingly.[32] Alongside struggles against dispossession, small scale farming beyond the dictates of capital, and in harmony with the natural environment, must feature in any revolutionary imaginary of a shared future.

I now bring this brief mapping of subordinate classes in the current conjuncture into conversation with various potentially progressive social forces. I will highlight potentialities of constructing a national-popular 'collective will' as well as the constraints posed by hegemonic middle-class conceptions.

Nation

The 'national question' in Pakistan, not unlike in many 'postcolonial informal empires', is extremely complex. The only modern nation-state which has experienced the secession of a majority ethnic group, Pakistan also has the dubious distinction of being a 'confessional state' which, like Israel, effectively designates many indigenous peoples and those outside the pale of the official ideology as colonial subjects.[33]

The militarisation of the ethnic peripheries under the shadow of imperialist war – accelerating dispossession and ecological breakdown – has predictably sharpened longstanding ethnic-national fault lines; PTM is the most potent recent articulation of resistance to racialised capitalism and colonial statecraft, but Sindhi, Baloch, Gilgit-Baltistani, Kashmiri, Siraiki and Muhajir nationalist assertion has also continued, and in some cases, intensified under the dual regimes of neoliberal globalisation and the war on terror.[34]

During the heyday of revolutionary internationalism, left-progressives and ethnic-nationalists closed ranks to form the National Awami Party that represented popular aspirations against the nexus of imperialism, the state and reactionary forces. Today too, it is within the ethnic peripheries that potentially 'ethical aspects' of desire for modernity are most likely to be hegemonised. Local propertied classes aside, the mass of people in the ethnic peripheries share a basic impulse for freedom and dignity whilst also being desirous of infrastructural development and service provision. But the political economy of patronage has to be navigated and ultimately transcended.

Moreover contemporary nationalist formations, the PTM most notable amongst them, are still prone to what Fanon termed the 'pitfalls of national consciousness'. Some segments of the Pashtun national movement, as well as other ethnic-nationalists, mirror the right by decrying the Punjabi 'other' as the source of oppression. Such a nationalist politics – which does not name the state, its imperial patrons and capital at large – simply reinforces the ideological binaries of the hegemonic regime.

At the onset of the war on terror, many a 'progressive' Pashtun nationalist welcomed the US invasion of Afghanistan under the pretext that Washington's military machine would bring right-wing extremism to heel. Some Sindhi and Baloch nationalists also courted support from western and other states to secure their 'freedom'. More generally, Pakistan's liberal intelligentsia, at various points in the post-9/11 conjuncture, put its lot in with the state and imperialist powers to defang 'extremism' and crush 'terrorists'.

The chaotic US departure from Afghanistan and reestablishment of Taliban rule in August 2021 demolished the ideological claims of the 'war on terror' and is likely to engender clear bifurcation of ethnic-nationalist forces in Pakistan. Some may continue to seek alliances with 'great powers' in cynical geopolitical games. Those who do not can be mobilised for a larger left-progressive effort to build a meaningful alternative to both state and capital, not to mention imperialism.

A recent study of the PTM argues that 'up-country migration of different ethnicities and real estate accumulation ... has laid the basis for new articulations of the national and urban question in Pakistan today'.[35] In Chapter 3, I shared my experience of organising in an Islamabad squatter settlement home to thousands of Pashtun migrant workers who had fled their war-torn homeland in the 1980s. Our work in I-11 *katchi abadi* sought to generate shared class sensibilities across *katchi abadi* residents from various ethnic-linguistic, caste and religious backgrounds. Arguably the most powerful articulation of 'universalising values' was in the form of solidarity expressed by Punjabi Christian towards the residents of I-11 (along with other Pashtuns designated as the proverbial 'other' under the counter-terrorism regime).

Punjabi Christians constitute the single biggest community of *katchi abadis* dwellers in the federal capital; theirs is a long history of exclusion and exploitation along class, caste and religious lines.[36] Largely confined to the status occupation of menial sweepers, they have been ghettoised through much of the modern period; in today's Pakistan, the vast majority of the country's Muslim population treats Punjabi Christians virtually as untouchables, unwilling to even countenance physical contact with them.

To forge solidarity between the Pashtun Muslims of I-11 *katchi abadi* and the Punjabi Christians scattered across many of the capital's informal settlements was an attempt, adapting Fanon, to 'make a step forward' and 'set afoot a new (wo)man'. The coming together of these diverse working-class communities for struggles against eviction also represented an alternative imaginary to a monolithic 'Punjab' that uniformly oppresses the ethnic peripheries.

A swathe of young middle-class subjects from centres and peripheries, historical and contemporary, were politicised by our ultimately failed attempt to resist eviction. They rejected the hegemonic signifiers of 'development' and 'counter-terrorism' while recognising the otherwise surplus masses that inhabited the settlement as *bona fide* political subjects. A similar cross-section of young people from Punjab and the ethnic peripheries alike were inspired by the person of Baba Jan, who spent almost a decade in jail for his peaceful activism in Gilgit-Baltistan. A son of GB's soil who rose to prominence on the frontline of local political causes,

Baba Jan speaks to the 'anticolonial desire' of young progressives across Pakistan. Such struggles and personas symbolise an embryonic alternative hegemony to the nexus of state and capital that, from colonial times till the present, has incessantly reproduced difference under regimes of uneven development.

Gender

There is arguably no single segment of Pakistan's 230 million people as oppressed and silenced as women (and girls). The combination of patriarchal violence and deeply imbibed sexism deprives a vast majority of women of their fundamental political subjecthood, even if digitalisation has at least facilitated agency for at least some confined to the walls of the home. Alongside trans and other non-binary peoples, upholding the dignity and meeting the basic material needs of women and girls must be at the forefront of any meaningful revolutionary project.

It is hence effectively a maxim that the classless subject is a feminist subject. Quite aside from what the future holds for the 'fourth wave' of Pakistani feminism, and the extent to which it becomes part of a larger left-progressive project, it is important to acknowledge that reactionary forces, and the religious right particularly so, have successfully mobilised women consistently and in much larger numbers than left-progressives. I noted in the introduction a growing body of scholarship that conceptualises young women joining religio-political organisations as a means of enhancing personal autonomy. Irrespective of the fact that these young women tend to reinforce many elements of the dominant patriarchal, militaristic and exclusionary hegemonic conception, they are far from passive subjects simply playing out a predesignated historical role.

In fact, insofar as the nuclear family is the primary cocoon within which the middle-class aspiration gestates, interrogating the crisis of care; feminisation of labour and poverty; and the politics of affect is essential to conceptualise a meaningful war of position all the way from the household to the highest levels of organised patriarchy.[37]

In concrete terms, this means both acknowledging and strategically challenging the political right's selective articulations of feminine subjectivity. Rashid, for instance, demonstrates how the Pakistani military mobilises women as symbols of sacrifice and purity for the proverbial 'nation', but at the same time how this trope of a 'loyal' woman is layered with contradiction.[38] Feminist principles must certainly inform a broader universalist politics beyond prevailing hegemonic notions of 'affect' and the patriarchal family. Yet rather than dramatic rupture, transcending the dominant patriarchal conception demands processual struggle that involves naming and then transforming established common sense.

In any case, the middle-class and youthful feminist subject will play a major role in shaping future political trajectories. Will she seek out and include other gendered subjects beyond the relatively individuated middle-class woman, and also articulate a 'personal politics' accordingly? This is not simply an abstract question, given that it is women and girls who bear a disproportionate impact of dispossession, war, and other brutalising aspects of the prevailing regime.

Earlier I discussed how the classical left intellectual of the 1950s – often with roots in the colonial educated classes – spoke for the 'peasant' and 'worker' even when organic relationships between the Party and these classes were few and far between. In the era of digitalised resistance, I would argue that a similar gulf exists between 'online' organisers and the mass of women who remain limited to 'offline' spaces.

Inasmuch as digitalised resistance is focused on the spectacular rather than the banal, most online organisers will continue to have limited contact with working-class women, and thereby unwittingly deny them the status of active political subjects. This is a challenge not only in the case of women, but the 'wretched of the earth' more broadly conceived. How subaltern segments are represented and who does the representing remain as important questions as ever.

For example, imagine a young Pakistani feminist employing a working-class woman as a domestic servant. That the former wilfully raises issues of patriarchal control and violence while also paying her servant a pittance is a contradiction that the feminist movement cannot overlook. Put differently, the struggle for hegemony *within* the feminist movement between liberal and socialist currents is part and parcel of the struggle to make the classless subject a feminist subject.

Finally, there is the task of pushing back against the tautological notion that only women can be feminists.[39] Of all of the drawn out and fraught struggles that constitute the revolutionary horizon of the classless subject, the challenge of men and boys imbibing feminist politics is arguably the most significant. Notwithstanding the eruption of the fourth wave of Pakistani feminism, patriarchal ideologies and practices remain deeply entrenched, Pakistani officialdom prone to outrageously sexist commentary and behaviour as a matter of course.[40]

To embody a revolutionary horizon that transcends patriarchal domination, the classless subject must commit to weaning out the 'toxic masculinity' inculcated in the vast majority of men and boys in Pakistani society. As many feminists have argued over the years, this includes transforming the sexual division of labour within the home itself, such that men and boys take on care work and related forms of emotional labour.

Ecology

The imperative of ecological regeneration can on its own be the basis of a universalist sensibility to shape politics for our times, especially in the historically imperialised zones of the world-system, which will bear the primary brunt of global warming and other manifestations of climate change. To the extent that what Chakrabarty calls a 'planetary consciousness' about the accelerating ecological crisis presently exists, however, it is centred primarily in the western heartlands of the world-system. A small segment of young people in countries like Pakistan exposed to cosmopolitan mores has to imbibe concern for the ecological question. But this is still an embryonic consciousness that broadly reproduces a 'merely environmental' perspective.[41]

In the final analysis, to meaningfully redress ecological breakdown is to acknowledge its broader political-economic foundations and alienated subjectivities within society at large. The case studies I have presented in this book – both where dispossession is proceeding apace, and where various forms of popular mobilisation push back against patriarchy, militarism, and neoliberal development – have illuminated the centrality and urgency of nature's despoilation. It follows, therefore, that a theory of revolutionary politics for the postcolony must preface the ecological crisis and a vision to redress it.

I have already noted that 'anticolonial desire' can undergird developmental imaginaries beyond neoliberal capitalism. This does not mean aping the postcolonial developmental state of the post WWII era that championed non-alignment, import substitution and at least a symbolic anti-imperialism. That developmental model is today simply incompatible with the sustenance of ecosystems and the innumerable forms of life, including humans, that the planet supports.[42]

In this sense alone, the question of technology is a crucial one. After all, the modernist project was founded upon the conviction that, armed with scientific knowledge, 'rational' man could finally understand and mould nature in the greater common good. Capitalist rationality and its destruction of the commons, especially in Europe's colonies, is now a matter of historical record, as is the way in which science and technology more specifically have been mobilised in the service of organised power.

More generally, the crisis of 'rational man' himself has reached its pinnacle. Scepticism about the prospect of humanity ever living up to the emancipatory imaginaries of modernity, as articulated by Marx and many others, is understandable, especially given the manner in which the political right has, in recent years, reneged on even hitherto globally agreed targets to curb warming, emissions and so on.

Yet the potentialities for science and technology to meet the needs of all peoples, while also regenerating nature, exist today. It is politics that lags behind. This is not to engage in any kind of techno-optimism. It is to assert the importance of guiding ethico-political principles for the mobilisation of technology. In the absence of alternative hegemonies, fear and desire will be mobilised to justify ever-greater centralisation of the state and corporate power in the face of climate change.

The prospect of an all-powerful Leviathan with unparalleled powers of surveillance – artificial intelligence (AI) and biotechnology even casting a shadow over human life – is reason enough to forge a hegemonic conception centring Marx's seminal ideas about 'species-being'. In the words of one interlocutor, the task of reconfiguring the relationship between humanity and nature is nothing less than a philosophical quest to accomplish 'the complete return of one to oneself as a human being'.[43]

The stakes over the greater common good, including the fate of future generations, are today higher than ever. Marx's dialectical understanding of labour as man's inscription of selfhood onto nature allows us to understand why capitalism has generated such a grave planetary imbalance. Only a distinct concept of selfhood, collective humanity and its relationship with nature can generate a distinct dialectic beyond capitalism. We need nothing less than need to foment an 'eco-political common sense that can orient a broadly shared project of transformation'.[44] As ever, the middle-class subject must be won over to this new common sense.

BUILDING A NATIONAL-POPULAR COLLECTIVE WILL

> Pre-capitalist populations, fighting to retain their territory and means of subsistence; 'surplus' masses, excluded from formal employment in the circuits of capitalist production; exploited manufacturing workers across rustbelt and sunbelt zones; new and old middle classes, increasingly encumbered with debt payments to the financial corporations – these constitute the potential social bases for contemporary critiques of the ruling capitalist order. Advance will almost certainly require alliances between them, and therefore the inter-articulation of their concerns. Which way – or ways – the new middle classes in Africa, Asia and Latin America swing will be a vital determinant.
>
> Goran Therborn[45]

Throughout this book, I have flagged the necessity of interrogating the social structures, mores and political subjectivities of the non-western postcolonial countries of South Asia and Sub-Saharan Africa autonomously *and* at the same time in dialectical conversation with the western heartlands of the capitalist world-system. My analytical claims, refracted through the specific case of Pakistan, are certainly not representative of the non-western world at large. Even accurately depicting the Pakistani case is a challenge, given how both historical and contemporary political-economic regimes have reproduced uneven developmental geographies and social differences alongside.

These caveats notwithstanding, I have identified what I believe to be the most vital points of departure for a particularistic postcolonial theory of politics with universalist overtones. Goran Therborn's suggestive analysis of the 'new masses' that could be the vanguard of global anti-capitalist politics in years to come offers a means of productive engagement with the thesis I have advanced in this book.

Insofar as Therborn identifies broad categories such as 'surplus' masses as being amongst the primary potential protagonists of a transformative politics, I am in agreement with him. However, a more nuanced interrogation of his propositions betrays a lack of attention to the specificity of the postcolonial condition. In particular, his characterisation of those 'fighting to retain their territory and means of subsistence' as 'pre-capitalist populations' is not consistent with my understanding of the various social segments in both historical centres and peripheries that are struggling against dispossession.

Not only are 'surplus' masses integrated into globalised circuits of capital, but it is also from within these subordinate classes, broadly conceived, that the middle-class subject in Africa, Asia and Latin America has emerged. Coercion alone is not sufficient to prop up regimes of dispossession; cooptation of working people whose livelihoods rely on land, water, forests and other natural resources is a crucial strategy of the 'land broker' state and private profiteers alike.

To be sure, the struggle for middle-class status in postcolonial South Asia and Sub Saharan Africa engages hundreds of millions of working people; displacing contemporary hegemony demands a tangible alternative to the politics of fear and desire. For such a conception to take root within the mass of working people, the following conditions must be met.

First, a 'national-popular' will must be profoundly internationalist in its essence. This internationalism must have strong roots within; I discussed above the imperative of addressing the 'national question' inside the territorial boundaries of the multi-ethnic postcolonial state. At a higher scale, the interconnectedness of the middle-class subject across the postcolonial world, both in its objective experience of global capitalism, and with regards to the subjectivities that are generated therein, can and must be asserted. This is especially important as the triumphalism of neoliberal globalisation gives way at least rhetorically to variations of economic nationalism.

Take the example of the 'vaccine nationalism' that came to light at the height of the COVID-19 pandemic. Billions in the historically imperialised zones of Asia, Africa and Latin America were deprived of access to vaccines that were surplus to requirements in western countries.[46] It is in response to such blatant expressions of neo-colonialism that an expansive national-popular will can be forged, unprecedented time-space compression afforded by digital networks providing at least some basis for a rehabilitated revolutionary internationalism.

Second, the national-popular must be articulated in an idiom that is explicitly distinguishable from the hate-mongering of the political right. This is not simply a question of displacing the politics of fear and desire *per se*, but recognising that the extreme ideological polarisations of our time cut across class, ethnic, gender, caste and religious fault lines, and that a long war of position entails winning over otherwise reactionary segments to an alternative hegemonic conception. Consciously or otherwise, progressives engaged in pitched battles with ideological adversaries can end up reproducing hateful caricatures and rhetoric that in fact provide further fuel for narrow nationalism, xenophobia and misogyny.

An emancipatory political horizon embodied by the classless subject cannot but transcend hate. Fanon reminds us:

> Hate is not inborn; it has to be constantly cultivated, to be brought into being, in conflict with more or less recognised guilt complexes. Hate demands existence, and he who hates has to show his hate in appropriate actions and behaviour; in a sense, he has to become hate.[47]

To articulate a transformative political idiom through 'appropriate actions and behaviour' that challenge hate can be both cause and consequence of an *active* consent and a national-popular will to match. As I have already noted, this calls for self-reflexivity, especially in the context of an increasingly digitalised field of politics that encourages maximal, and often deeply polarising positions.

Third, progressives must engage with the question of religious faith, which, in most parts of South Asia and Sub Saharan Africa, significantly shapes everyday common sense. I noted in Chapter 4 how Pakistan's political left has long been burdened with propagandist claims of its irreligiosity, particularly after Pakistan became the staging ground of *jihad* waged against 'godless' Soviet forces in Afghanistan.

The accession to state power of the Hindu Right in India and Sinhala-Buddhist supremacism in Sri Lanka, among other examples, confirm the centrality of religion in sustaining contemporary hegemony across South Asia. Moreover, in the face of growing inequality and repression, these ideological and political formations give credence to Marx's often misinterpreted assertion about '[r]*eligious* suffering [as] the *expression* of real suffering and a *protest* against real suffering. Religion is the sigh of the oppressed creature, the heart of a heartless world, and the soul of soulless conditions'.[48]

It is telling that the almost millenarian commitment of left revolutionaries of the 20th century is today expressed almost exclusively by the foot soldiers of the religious right. As I noted above with respect to the right's mobilisation of women, rather than simply decry the appeal of religious symbols and practices, it is far more useful to consider how an alternative hegemonic conception can be formulated that displaces exclusionary and oppressive ideas and practices while at the same time recognising the religious affinities of large segments of society. The obvious example from which to learn in this regard is liberation theology in Latin America, but indigenous movements and figures from the past can and must be mobilised.

Between the first world war and the decolonisation of India, Muslim clerics like Ubaidullah Sindhi espoused eclectic ideologies with a socialist horizon. Even more recently, Pakistan's first elected government espoused a somewhat confused 'Islamic socialism' as its guiding ideology. That regime's attempt to reconcile religion as state ideology with left-imaginaries was misguided, but it is precisely the fact that religion has been weaponised by imperialism, state and reactionary forces that compels progressives to engage with the vexed question of its place in an alternative hegemonic conception.

I have written elsewhere about the insularity and increasing elitism of 'secularists' in contemporary Pakistan, in comparison to which the religious right has projected itself as connected to working people.[49] The actual form and content of an alternative hegemonic conception that incorporates religious subjectivities can only be established in and through struggle, but it is first and foremost necessary to acknowledge this imperative. Indeed, as the interlocking crises facing humanity intensify, and postcolonial countries like Pakistan especially so, the 'sigh of the oppressed creature' is likely to have a spiritual imprint of some kind. To turn the subjective experience and understanding of religious belief away from fear and desire, state nationalism and 'othering' is, therefore, as significant a challenge as any other.

Epilogue

> We do not say to the world: Cease your struggles, they are foolish; we will give you the true slogan of struggle. We merely show the world what it is really fighting for, and consciousness is something that it *has to* acquire, even if it does not want to.
>
> Karl Marx (1843) Letter to Arnold Ruge[1]

Lenin famously said that without a revolutionary theory there can be no revolutionary movement. While today's world is in many ways unrecognisable from the one in which Lenin and his Bolshevik Party conceptualised revolutionary politics and constructed the world's first socialist state, an appeal to the essence of Lenin's simple formulation informs the writing of this book.

Seen through the gaze of the western political and intellectual mainstream, the contemporary rule of capital is both exacerbating social polarisation and emboldening reactionary forces, the global financial crisis of 2006-8 having triggered the implosion of the ideological and political formation that is progressive neoliberalism. But seen from the historic peripheries of the world-system, where colonial statecraft and the logic of capital have combined to expropriate ever-larger numbers of working people in often violent ways, and pillage nature alongside, the interlocking crises that afflict humanity appear even more grave.

The acute brutalisation generated by imperialist wars, globalised monopoly-finance capital, interconnected regimes of dispossession and patriarchal/racialised social structures have precipitated significant 'digitalised' resistance, as a young generation of politicised middle-class subjects uses social media platforms to call attention to class, state, imperialist, gendered and other forms of power. But this digitalised resistance does not always correspond to organic links with the proverbial 'workers' and 'peasants' that bear the brunt of contemporary regimes of dispossession. Meanwhile, pitched online battles that left-progressives wage with reactionaries and, indeed, one another, underline a lack of reflexivity about the contradictory aspects of digitalisation. As such, the prevailing dynamics of digitalised resistance often impede conceptualisation of a transformative politics for times to come.

Principled voices of dissent will continue to resist the excesses of organised power, and in so doing contribute to politicisation of subsequent generations of young people. But in the absence of an alternative hegemonic conception, the politics of fear and desire will continue to be propagated, passive consent generated from the youthful middle-class subject that, for all intents and purposes, represents the widest cross-section of postcolonial society.

It is under this backdrop that I invoke Lenin. A substantive political theory that accords primary to the postcolonial condition will be shaped further in and through struggle – my purpose in this book has been to identify the major structuring factors that are shaping political subjectivity, and which must be accounted for in any political theory that envisions a future humanity in concert with nature.

A number of contemporary left thinkers and practitioners emphasise that progressive thinking and movements of resistance must go beyond critique and articulate a viable vision of a post-capitalist social order. I concur that brutalising systemic logics will persist until the middle-class subjects that animate the hegemonic order are won over by an alternative 'ethico-political' conception which adequately appeals to their sensibilities.

This imperative has precipitated a series of treatises about futures beyond capitalism. Some are premised on a techno-optimism in which capitalism is gradually transcended; others offer imaginaries of a 'corpo-syndicalist' world in which share markets and commercial banks cease to exist.[2] As with much contemporary theorising on the left, such treatises, while extremely compelling, pay scant attention to the objective-subjective realities of most of the world, that is, the postcolonial regions of South Asia and Sub-Saharan Africa.

To draw out this point I wish to return to the imaginary of gated housing communities, which I argued in Chapter 1 are amongst the most idealised symbols of hegemonic middle-class subjectivity in the current conjuncture. Assume that the socio-spatial configuration of the gated housing communities is extended to its limits, both with regards to nature and the mass of working people that neither possess the cultural capital nor the purchasing power to acquire membership therein. The result is an elite ghetto walled in from all sides from a wasteland in which large segments of humanity struggle to secure the basic necessities of life, including water and air.

In this dystopic imaginary, a combination of organised state power and private militias maintain security for the elite ghetto, as well as the islands of development that churn out energy supplies necessary for the rich and powerful to sustain their lifestyles. Meanwhile, the mass of humanity is largely surplus to requirements, its only 'productive' role – in the eyes of capital – being the performance of slave labour to keep the development wheel churning. Consider further fully developed digitalised surveillance systems, artificial intelligence and genetic engineering shaping a world that has been devastated by climate breakdown and ensuing water/energy wars.

Dystopic representations of the future have of course animated commercial films and books for decades. Even if one does not quite buy into Hollywood-style depictions, it is indubitable that contemporary regimes of dispossession are microcosmic examples of what the entire social landscape could resemble in the not so distant future.

The COVID-19 pandemic has accelerated the deepening of what can literally be called a survival-of-the-fittest mentality. We are already seeing the emergence of a global common sense – and forms of mobility – sustained by a 'global police state' that enforces our own fear of contact with other humans, epitomised by artefacts like 'vaccine passports'. The cutting edge research of epidemiologists like Rob Wallace warns that further and far more grievous public health disasters are imminently likely, thus making the metaphorical elite ghetto an even more palpable idea.[3] It is thus that we must contemplate the prospects of a universal descent into barbarism.

In invoking barbarism, I am calling attention not only to the prospect of elite ghettos dotting the world's landscape while 'surplus' masses languish beyond their walls. I am also signalling the urgency of interrogating the brutalising processes of subjectivation taking humanity as a whole closer and closer to this precipice. The challenge of imagining and then forging a national-popular including both the middle-class subject and surplus masses alike demands that we confront the increasingly brutalised subjectivities proliferating in postcolonial and, indeed, many other societies of the world.

Subaltern men, women and children are the foot soldiers of racism, sexism, caste-ism and other manifestations of organised power in the nooks and crannies of society, not to mention the loyal citizen-subjects that prop up state nationalism more generally. The far-right benefits from and continually reinforces hate-mongering and everyday violence. In such an environment, the working masses are more likely to compete against one another to survive, rather than cooperate, as and when major climate breakdown events gather pace. Recall that South Asia is the world's most vulnerable region to such eventualities.

This is why it is essential to theorise a war of position in which subjective transformation is accorded central importance. This is not to discount the prospects of a viable left-wing political project taking state power and enacting meaningful policy shifts in individual South Asian or African countries in the current conjuncture – the Latin American 'pink tide' is an example of a somewhat successful war of manoeuvre during the regime of neoliberal globalisation. Burgeoning contradictions within dominant class coalitions and state establishments that have come to the fore as neoliberal hegemony has faltered have certainly given wind to political forces beyond the 'extreme centre'. These contradictions are politicising young people in countries like Pakistan, some of them shifting to the left.

Whether potential victories in the electoral realm can contribute to the deepening of imaginaries such as the 'classless subject' is nevertheless a strategic question that varies with context. In any case, the 'digital party' with which many young people are putting in their lot, punctuated by the larger-than-life role of the 'hyper-leader', is yet to be proven a vehicle of substantive social transformation.[4]

Could it be that insurrectionary politics will, in the not too distant future, have to be shielded from not only the internal dynamics of 'the digital', but also the ever enhancing capacity of the state and Big Tech to surveil? Might we need to eventually return to political collectivities that remain 'off the grid'? Will the imperative of human survival be pitted against the proverbial machine that the human intellect itself has spawned?

These are just some of the many outstanding 'big' questions confronting left-progressives as practical experiments proceed apace in the realm of struggle. In any case, it is necessary to articulate at least as much what we are 'for' as what we are 'against'. This means a conception of 'development' and the 'commons' that is inclusive rather than based on the generation of 'surplus' masses. I have focused in this book on the subjective element rather than posit the specifics of an alternative political-economic structure in Pakistan, and indeed, the planet at large.

I do not claim that this is anything more than a skeletal offering. I have posited only principles – symbolised by euphemisms like 'new (wo)man' – required to transcend hate. Concrete articulations of exactly how this revolutionary subjectivity can be inculcated will be expressed in the struggle.

It bears recounting here that the philosopher-practitioners that I have invoked most in this book, Antonio Gramsci and Frantz Fanon, conceptualised revolutionary subjectivities in similarly general rather than specific registers. Even more significantly, Gramsci was a 'theoretician of the defeat of socialism' and never really provided much indication of how what he called 'good sense' would emerge from the womb of actually existing 'common sense'.[5] Meanwhile, Fanon's most prescient writings brought into focus how the national bourgeoisie would doom the 20th-century project of revolutionary internationalism.

Despite living through a period of intense reaction, we can now name the many burgeoning contradictions that engulf the neoliberal project. If the yearning for something different has been prominent in the western heartlands of the world-system since at least the events of 2006–2008, the COVID-19 pandemic has signalled the increasing volatility of what I have called the hegemonic politics of fear and desire in postcolonial South Asia and Africa. The vaunted middle-class subject that has embodied the 'rise' of South Asia and Africa since the 1990s can and must be mobilised to an alternative hegemonic conception that centres the subjectivities of 'surplus' genders, castes, religious communities, ethnic nations and, more generally, the mass of working people.

Tending to this most urgent political task, while reflexively immersing ourselves in real struggles against dispossession, war and everyday violence, is the sufficient condition to redress endless crisis, and thereby transcend the logic of capital, colonial statecraft and hate.

Notes

INTRODUCTION

1. Gillian Hart (2020) 'Why did it take so long? Trump-Bannonism in a global conjunctural frame'. *Geografiska Annaler: Series B, Human Geography 102* (3) pp. 239–266.
2. Francis Fukuyama. *The end of history and the last man* (New York: Simon and Schuster, 2006).
3. Manuel Castells. *The rise of the network society* (New Jersey: John Wiley & Sons, 2011).
4. Samir Amin (2000) 'Economic globalism and political universalism: conflicting issues?'. *Journal of World-Systems Research 6* (3) pp. 582–622.
5. Wendy Brown. *Undoing the demos: Neoliberalism's stealth revolution* (Cambridge: MIT Press, 2015).
6. Ranabir Sammaddar. *Karl Marx and the Postcolonial Age* (London: Palgrave-Macmillan, 2017) p. 3.
7. I borrow the term from Harvey whose book does not interrogate postcolonial social formations *per se*. See David Harvey. *Marx, capital, and the madness of economic reason*. (New York: Oxford University Press, 2017).
8. Rohit Inani (2021) 'How a year of Covid-19 financially dented India's middle class'. *Indiaspend*. www.indiaspend.com/covid-19/how-a-year-of-covid-19-financially-dented-indias-middle-class-770838 (Accessed September 2021).
9. The almost complete lack of regulation in practices of industrial animal farming and many related capitalist sectors that gave rise to the novel coronavirus suggest ominously that COVID-19 is likely to be just the tip of the iceberg. See Rob Wallace, Alex Liebman, Luis F. Chaves and Rodrick Wallace (2020) 'COVID-19 and circuits of capital'. *Monthly Review 72* (1) May.
10. Tariq Ali. *The extreme centre: a second warning* (London and New York: Verso Books, 2015).
11. See Nancy Fraser. *The old is dying and the new cannot be born: From progressive neoliberalism to Trump and beyond* (New York and London: Verso Books, 2019). I do not engage in this book with the many important debates on the evolving class composition of

so-called 'advanced' western societies. Suffice it to say, following Samir Amin, that the 'Golden Age' of post-WWII growth in the 'Imperialist Triad' of North America, western Europe, and Japan facilitated upward mobility and broadly 'middle-class' lifestyles for a broad cross-section of those regions' populations.

12. Christian Fuchs. *Digital demagogue: Authoritarian capitalism in the age of Trump and Twitter* (London: Pluto Press, 2018) p. 289.
13. See, for example, Christian Fuchs. *Rereading Marx in the age of digital capitalism* (London: Pluto Press, 2019); Wendy Brown, Peter E. Gordon and Max Pensky. *Authoritarianism: Three inquiries in critical theory* (Chicago: University of Chicago Press, 2018); Dylan Riley (2018) 'What is Trump?' *New Left Review 114*. November–December.
14. See, for example, Aaron Bastani. *Fully automated luxury communism* (New York and London: Verso Books, 2019); John Bellamy Foster, Brett Clark and Richard York. *The ecological rift: Capitalism's war on the earth* (New York: NYU Press, 2011); Guy Standing. *Plunder of the commons* (London: Penguin Books, 2019).
15. Commentary in the media mainstream has been much more prolific, but explicitly political *theory* far less so. Exceptions include Achin Vanaik (2018) 'India's two hegemonies'. *New Left Review 112* pp. 29–59; Nicole Curato (ed). *A Duterte reader: Critical essays on Rodrigo Duterte's early presidency* (Ithaca: Cornell University Press, 2017); Cihan Tugal. *The fall of the Turkish model: How the Arab uprisings brought down Islamic liberalism* (New York and London: Verso Books, 2016). See also the August 2021 *GeoForum* Special Volume (2021) entitled 'Authoritarian Developmentalism' edited by Murat Arsel, Fikret Adaman and Alfredo Saad-Filho.
16. Jean Comaroff and John Comaroff (2012) 'Theory from the South: Or, how Europe is evolving toward Africa'. *Anthropological Forum* 22 (2) p. 113. Also compelling in this regard is Sammaddar's (2017, pp. 31–35) reading of the now central importance of meaningful knowledge-production and theory of previously orientalised/instrumentalised colonial peripheries.
17. India, Pakistan, Nigeria, Tanzania, Democratic Republic of Congo, Niger, Uganda and Ethiopia are projected to be responsible for 50% of all the growth in human population between now and 2100. See Dipesh Chakrabarty. *The climate of history in a planetary age* (Chicago: University of Chicago Press, 2021) p. 98.
18. Joel Wainwright and Geoff Mann (2013) 'Climate leviathan'. *Antipode* 45 (1) p. 11.
19. Jodi Dean. *The communist horizon* (London and New York: Verso Books, 2012).

20. Durr-e-Nayab (2011) 'Estimating the middle class in Pakistan'. *The Pakistan Development Review* 50 (1) pp. 1–28.
21. Branko Milanovic. *Capitalism, Alone: The Future of the System That Rules the World* (Cambridge: Harvard University Press, 2019) p. 3.
22. Hadas Weiss. *We have never been middle class* (New York and London: Verso, 2019).
23. See Branko Milanovic. *Global inequality: A new approach for the age of globalization* (Cambridge: Harvard University Press, 2016); Maryam Aslany (2019) 'The Indian middle class, its size, and urban-rural variations'. *Contemporary South Asia* 27 (2) pp. 196–213; Abebe Shimeles and Mthuli Ncube (2015) 'The making of the middle-class in Africa: Evidence from DHS data'. *The Journal of Development Studies* 51 (2) pp. 178–193.
24. See Leela Fernandes. *India's new middle class: Democratic politics in an era of economic reform* (Minneapolis: University of Minnesota Press, 2006); Amira Baviskar and Raka Ray (eds). *Elite and everyman: The cultural politics of the Indian middle classes* (London: Taylor & Francis, 2020); Ammara Maqsood. *The new Pakistani middle class* (Cambridge: Harvard University Press, 2017); Helmuth Lange and Lars Meier (eds). *The new middle classes: globalizing lifestyles, consumerism and environmental concern* (Heidelberg: Springer, 2009); Lean Kroeker, David O'Kane and Tabea Scharrer (eds) *Middle Classes in Africa* (London: Palgrave-Macmillan, 2018).
25. Pierre Bourdieu. *Distinction: A social critique of the judgment of taste* (Cambridge: Harvard University Press, 1984) p. 106.
26. There has always been a palpable gap between the abstract conceptual claims of *neoliberalism* and the highly politicised and 'unfree' markets that characterise *neoliberalisation* in practice. See David Harvey. *A brief history of neoliberalism* (New York: Oxford University Press, 2007).
27. Rosa Luxemburg. *The accumulation of capital* (Abingdon and New York: Routledge, 2003) p. 322.
28. Siddharta Deb. *The beautiful and the damned: A portrait of the new India* (London: Penguin Books, 2012).
29. Milanovic, 2016, p. 202. In the Indian context, 'the ideational force of "middle-class" status harnesses the aspirational dispositions of less privileged sections of the middle classes even though these segments are structurally constrained by the reproduction of socio-economic inequality'. See Leela Fernandes. '*Rethinking the dominant proprietary classes: India's middle classes and the reproduction of inequality*'. In Elizabeth Chatterjee and Matthew McCartney (eds) *Class and*

conflict: Revisiting Pranab Bardhan's political economy of India (Delhi: Oxford University Press, 2019) p. 194.

30. Ronald Munck (2013) 'The Precariat: a view from the South'. *Third World Quarterly 34* (5) pp. 747–762.
31. Joel Wainwright and Geoff Mann. *Climate leviathan: A political theory of our planetary future* (London and New York: Verso Books, 2018).
32. Najeeb A. Jan. *The metacolonial state: Pakistan, critical ontology, and the biopolitical horizons of political Islam* (New Jersey: John Wiley & Sons, 2019).
33. Natalya Naqvi (2018) 'Finance and industrial policy in unsuccessful developmental states: The case of Pakistan'. *Development and Change 49* (4) pp. 1064–1092.
34. Tahir H. Naqvi. 'Private satellite media and the geopolitics of moderation in Pakistan'. In Shakuntala Banaji (ed) *South Asian Media cultures: Audiences, representations, contexts* (London and New York: Anthem Press, 2010) pp. 109–122.
35. Ayyaz Mallick (2017) 'Beyond "domination without hegemony": Passive revolution(s) in Pakistan'. *Studies in Political Economy 98* (3) p. 254.
36. Ishtiaq Ahmed. *Pakistan the garrison state: origins, evolution, consequences, 1947–2011* (Karachi: Oxford University Press, 2013).
37. Meekal Ahmed. 'An economic crisis state?'. In Maleeha Lodhi (ed) *Pakistan: Beyond the crisis state* (Karachi: Oxford University Press, 2011), pp. 169–200.
38. Maleeha Lodhi. 'Beyond the crisis state'. In Lodhi (ed), 2011, p. 67.
39. Electricity provision remained a state monopoly until the mid-1990s when the World Bank presided over a classic neoliberal restructuring process under the guise of reducing inefficiencies in the power market. Production of power was separated from distribution, so called Private Power Producers (PPPs) given control over the former, with public enterprises left only with control over the latter. By the mid-2000s, this model of 'public–private' provision of electricity fell woefully out of sync with consumer demand leading to widespread blackouts – or 'loadshedding'. For detailed analysis of Pakistan's power sector and WB led reforms, see Ijlal Naqvi (2016) 'Pathologies of development practice: Higher order obstacles to governance reform in the Pakistani electrical power sector'. *The Journal of Development Studies 52* (7) pp. 950–964.
40. Aasim Sajjad Akhtar (2010) 'Pakistan: Crisis of a frontline state'. *Journal of Contemporary Asia 40* (1) pp. 105–122.

41. Marta Bolognani (2010) 'Virtual protest with tangible effects? Some observations on the media strategies of the 2007 Pakistani anti-Emergency movement'. *Contemporary South Asia 18* (4) pp. 401–412.
42. Virender S. Kalra (2018) 'Student organising in Pakistan: New spaces for articulating old political forces'. *Panjab University Research Journal (Arts) XLV* (1) January–June p. 4.
43. Quoted from Vasant Natajaran (2016) 'An ode to English'. *The Hindu* 26 January.
44. For an interesting exposition of a less influential but no less important 'Urdu middle-class milieu' that espoused an insular and 'anti-societal' politics, see Markus Daechsel. *The politics of self-expression: The Urdu Middleclass Milieu in mid-twentieth century India and Pakistan* (Oxfordshire: Routledge, 2006).
45. Frantz Fanon. *The wretched of the earth* (London: McGibbon and Kee, 1965) pp. 99–100.
46. See Vivek Chibber. *Postcolonial theory and the specter of capital* (New York and London: Verso, 2013); Christof Dejung, David Motadel, and Jürgen Osterhammel (eds) *The global bourgeoisie: The rise of the middle classes in the age of empire* (Princeton: Princeton University Press, 2019).
47. Aime Cesaire. *Discourse on colonialism* (New York: New York University Press, 2001) pp. 31–40.
48. Pranab Bardhan. *The political economy of development in India: Expanded edition with an epilogue on the political economy of reform in India* (Delhi: Oxford University Press, 1999). A recently published volume insightfully recapitulates Bardhan's main arguments and analyses class and state formation in the ensuing decades. See Elizabeth Chatterjee and Matthew McCartney (eds). *Class and conflict: Revisiting Pranab Bardhan's political economy of India* (Delhi: Oxford University Press, 2019).
49. Aasim Sajjad Akhtar (2019) 'The overdeveloped Alavian legacy'. In S. Akbar Zaidi and Matthew McCartney (eds) *New perspectives on Pakistan's political economy: State, class and social change* (Cambridge: Cambridge University Press, 2019) pp. 55–74.
50. Mahmood Mamdani. *Citizen and subject: Contemporary Africa and the legacy of late colonialism* (Princeton: Princeton University Press, 2018).
51. Ramachandra Guha. *India after Gandhi: The history of the world's largest democracy* (Basingstoke: Pan Macmillan. 2017).
52. Paula R. Newberg. *Judging the state: Courts and constitutional politics in Pakistan* (Cambridge: Cambridge University Press, 2002).

53. Ammara Maqsood. *The new Pakistani middle class* (Cambridge: Harvard University Press, 2017) p. 21.
54. From the government press note reprinted in *The New York Times*, 8 October 1958.
55. Salman R. Sheikh. *The genesis of Baloch nationalism: Politics and ethnicity in Pakistan, 1947–1977* (Oxfordshire: Routledge, 2018) p. 36.
56. See Ayesha Jalal. *Democracy and authoritarianism in South Asia: A comparative and historical perspective* (Cambridge: Cambridge University Press, 1995); Taylor C. Sherman, William Gould and Sarah Ansari (eds). *From subjects to citizens: Society and the everyday state in India and Pakistan, 1947–1970* (Delhi: Cambridge University Press, 2014).
57. It is worth being reminded that Gramsci's ruminations in prison were motivated by a desire to explain why the Italian left failed to foment popular revolution despite the Communist Party (PCI) appearing to be on the cusp of taking state power in 1919–1920. His prison writings underscored the need for an idiom of politics that resonated with and yet could transcend historically rooted cultural forms. This was the sufficient condition for a broad cross-section of popular forces to coalesce around a national-popular project in an acutely uneven social formation.
58. See Ali Raza. *Revolutionary pasts: Communist internationalism in colonial India* (Cambridge: Cambridge University Press, 2020) p. 3. Raza painstakingly demonstrates how revolutionary internationalism as embodied in the Ghadar, Lascar and Khilafat movement in India was both cause and consequence of the personal journeys of Indian revolutionaries across the early 20th century imperialised world. Importantly, 'middle-class' students and intellectuals were heavily represented in the case studies he documents.
59. Fanon, 1965, p. 52.
60. Kamran A. *Communism in Pakistan: Politics and class activism 1947–1972* (London: Bloomsbury Publishing, 2015).
61. Saadia Toor. *The State of Islam: culture and cold war politics in Pakistan.* (London: Pluto Press, 2011).
62. Kamran A. Ali (2011) 'Communists in a Muslim Land: Cultural Debates in Pakistan's Early Years'. *Modern Asian Studies* 45 (3) p. 518.
63. Jean Luc Nancy and Frank Ruda (2017) 'Lenin and Electricity'. *Crisis and Critique* 4 (2) pp. 356–361.
64. Kamran A. Ali (2005). 'The strength of the street meets the strength of the state: The 1972 labor struggle in Karachi'. *International Journal of Middle East Studies* 37 (1) pp. 83–107.

65. Noaman G. Ali (2020) 'Agrarian class struggle and state formation in post-colonial Pakistan, 1959–1974: Contingencies of Mazdoor Kisan Raj'. *Journal of Agrarian Change* 20 (2) pp. 270–288.
66. Two recently published Urdu autobiographies by left intellectuals and political leaders through the tumult of the Cold War years bear out the extent of sectarianism within the left's ranks. Pro-Chinese and pro-Russian factions jostled for influence, with Trotskyites joining the fray in the 1980s. See Chaudhry Fateh Mohammad. *Jo hum pe guzri* (Lahore: Sanjh Publications, 2016); Abid Hasan Minto. *Apni jang rahe gi* (Lahore: Sanjh Publications, 2016).
67. Aijaz Ahmad (1978) 'Democracy and dictatorship in Pakistan'. *Journal of Contemporary Asia* 8 (4) pp. 477–512.
68. Michael Kalecki. *Selected essays on the economic growth of the socialist and the mixed economy* (Cambridge: Cambridge University Press, 1972).
69. Aasim Sajjad Akhtar. *The politics of common sense: state, society and culture in Pakistan* (Cambridge: Cambridge University Press, 2018).
70. Sudipta Kaviraj (1984) 'A critique of the passive revolution'. *Economic and Political Weekly* 23 (45/47) pp. 2429–2444.
71. Jeffrey Witsoe 'Caste and democratization in postcolonial India: an ethnographic examination of lower caste politics in Bihar'. *Democratization* 19 (2) p. 7.
72. See Partha Chatterjee. *The politics of the governed: reflections on popular politics in most of the world* (New York: Columbia University Press, 2004); Jeffrey Witsoe. *Democracy against development: Lower-caste politics and political modernity in postcolonial India* (Chicago: University of Chicago Press, 2013); Asef Bayat. *Life as politics: How ordinary people change the Middle East* (Stanford: Stanford University Press, 2013).
73. Chantal Mouffe. *For a left populism* (New York and London: Verso, 2018).
74. See Jean Francois Bayart. *The state in Africa: the politics of the belly* (Cambridge: Polity, 2009). Also useful in delineating the intricacies of 'the political' in postcolonial Sub-Saharan Africa is the concept of 'extraversion'. Distinguishing between 'extraversion' and the *dependencia* school which arguably made much more deterministic, and, ultimately, unviable claims about the totalising nature of the capitalist world-system, Bayart and Ellis note that postcolonial ruling blocs and the larger dynamics of the polity have to be understood in terms of 'the creation and capture of a rent generated by dependency and which functions as a historical matrix of inequality, political centralisation and social struggle'. See Jean Francois Bayart and Stephen

Ellis (2000) 'Africa in the world: a history of extraversion'. *African Affairs* 99 (395) p. 222.

75. In a classic text, Zaman demonstrated how militant Sunni organisations backed by hitherto weak commercial castes challenged dominant landed power in the Punjabi province of Jhang, with the sectarian card proving particularly effective on account of the latter's Shi'a background. See Muhammad Qasim Zaman (1998) 'Sectarianism in Pakistan: The radicalization of Shi 'i and Sunni identities'. *Modern Asian Studies* 32 (3) pp. 689–716.
76. Oskar Verkaaik. *Migrants and militants: fun and urban violence in Pakistan* (Princeton: Princeton University Press, 2004); Humeira Iqtidar. Secularizing Islamists?: Jama'at-e-Islami and Jama'at-ud-Da'wa in urban Pakistan (Chicago and London: Chicago University Press, 2011); Sadaf Ahmad. *Transforming faith: the story of Al-Huda and Islamic revivalism among urban Pakistani women* (Syracuse: Syracuse University Press, 2009).
77. S. Akbar Zaidi (2005) 'State, military and social transition: Improbable future of democracy in Pakistan'. *Economic and Political Weekly* 40 (49) pp. 5175.
78. For a useful summary of how this debate has evolved over the years, see Subir Sinha and Rashmi Varma (2017) 'Marxism and postcolonial theory: what's left of the debate'. *Critical Sociology* 43 (4–5) pp. 545–558.
79. Vivek Chibber (2006) 'On the decline of class analysis in South Asian studies'. *Critical Asian Studies* 38 (4) pp. 357–387.
80. Aijaz Ahmad (1997) 'Postcolonial theory and the "post" condition'. *Socialist Register* 33 p. 357.
81. Ravinder Kaur (2018) 'World as commodity: Or, how the "third world" became an "emerging market"'. *Comparative Studies of South Asia, Africa and the Middle East* 38 (2) pp. 384, 393.
82. Walden Bello, Bill Rau and Shea Cunningham. *Dark Victory: The US, Structural Adjustment, and Global Poverty* (London: Pluto Press, 1994).
83. Partha Chatterjee. *I am the people: Reflections on popular sovereignty today* (Columbia: Columbia University Press, 2019).
84. Ravinder Kaur (2016). '"I am India shining": The investor-citizen and the indelible icon of good times'. *The Journal of Asian Studies* 75 (3) p. 629.
85. Kalyan Sanyal. *Rethinking capitalist development: Primitive accumulation, governmentality and post-colonial capitalism* (Delhi: Routledge, 2014).
86. Ibid., p. 53.

87. I should note here that Marx did not conceptualise the 'reserve army of labour' and 'surplus populations' as the same. See Nick Bernards and Susanne Soederberg (2020) 'Relative surplus populations and the crises of contemporary capitalism: Reviving, revisiting, recasting'. *Geoforum*. Doi: 10.1016/j.geoforum.2020.12.009 (Accessed September 2021).
88. Partha Chatterjee (2008) 'Democracy and economic transformation in India'. *Economic and Political Weekly* 43 (16) p. 55.
89. Sammadar (2017, p. 154–165) argues that Sanyal's argument betrays a 'fetish of the informal'.
90. Kaur, 2016, p. 645. See also Nandini Gooptu (ed). *Enterprise culture in neoliberal India: Studies in youth, class, work and media* (Delhi: Routledge, 2013).
91. My critical reading of Sanyal resonates to a significant extent with the arguments made in Vinay Gidwani and Joel Wainwright (2014) 'On capital, not-capital, and development: after Kalyan Sanyal'. *Economic and Political Weekly XLIX* (34) pp. 40–47. See also Anirbhan Dasgupta (2021) 'Peasant production in India: How the "need economy" facilitates accumulation'. *Development and Change* 52 (2) pp. 217–240.
92. Sammadar, 2017, p. 50.
93. Chakrabarty, 2021, p. 45.
94. Lucia Michelutti and Barbara Harris-White. *The wild east: criminal political economies in South Asia* (London: UCL Press, 2019).
95. Samir Amin (2018) 'The communist manifesto, 170 years later'. *Monthly Review.* October.

1 THE INTEGRAL STATE

1. Charles Tilly. 'Warmaking and statemaking as organised crime'. In Peter Evans, Dietrich Rueschemeyer and Theda Skocpol. *Bringing the state back in* (Cambridge: Cambridge University Press, 1985) pp. 169–187.
2. It is well established that Gramsci borrowed the concept of hegemony from Lenin, developing it further in the *Prison Notebooks*. See Peter Thomas. *The Gramscian moment: philosophy, hegemony and Marxism* (Leiden: Brill, 2009).
3. Concepts like 'political society' and 'state' are deployed by Gramsci in often confusing ways. On occasion, he collapses the two terms entirely, while on others they represent distinct domains.
4. See Neelam Srivastava and Baidik Bhattacharya (eds). *The Postcolonial Gramsci* (Oxford: Routledge, 2012); Michael Ekers, Gillian Hart,

Stefan Kipfer and Alex Loftus (eds). *Gramsci: Space, nature, politics* (New York: John Wiley & Sons, 2012); Tom Nairn also offers the insight that 'he was a product of the west's most remote periphery, and of conditions which, half a century later, it became fashionable to call "Third World"'. See Tom Nairn, 'Antonu Su Gobbu'. In Anne Showstack Sassoon (ed). *Approaches to Gramsci. Writers and Readers* (London: Writers and Readers Co-op Society, 1982) pp. 159–179.

5. Thomas, 2009, p. 22. The concepts of 'Integral State' and 'hegemonic apparatus' come together as follows: '[I]f the concept of the integral state seeks to delineate the forms and modalities by which a given class stabilises and makes more or less enduring its institutional-political power in political society, the concept of a "hegemonic apparatus" attempts to chart the ways in which it ascends to power through the intricate network of social relationships of civil society' (Thomas, 2009, p. 224).
6. A lively debate on 'extractivism' and 'neo-extractivism' has animated critical theorists of Latin American development for some years now. For a useful summary of these debates, see Hans-Jurgen Burchardt and Kristina Dietz (2014) '(Neo-)extractivism – a new challenge for development theory from Latin America'. *Third World Quarterly* 35 (3) pp. 468–486.
7. For an incisive exposition of the Gramscian dialectic in conversation with other critical theories, see Gillian Hart. (2018) 'Relational comparison revisited: Marxist postcolonial geographies in practice'. *Progress in Human Geography* 42 (3) pp. 371–394.
8. The UNDP has also identified 'elite privilege' as a major structuring fact of Pakistan's political economy, the richest 20% of the population controlling almost half the country's wealth, even asserting that a 'social movement' is necessary to dismantle militarised, class structures. See www.aljazeera.com/news/2021/4/13/elite-privilege-consumes-17-4bn-of-pakistans-economy-undp
9. Rosita Armytage. *Big capital in an unequal world: The micropolitics of wealth in Pakistan* (New York: Berghahn Books, 2020) p. 13.
10. Stephen M. Lyon. *Political kinship in Pakistan: Descent, marriage, and government stability* (Washington DC: Lexington Books, 2019).
11. Ali Cheema, Hasan Javid and Farooq Naseer (2013) 'Dynastic politics in Punjab: Facts, myths and their implications'. *Institute of Development and Economic Alternatives Working Paper* (01–13). https://ideaspak.org/wp-content/files_mf/1551780853Dynastic PoliticsinPunjabFactMythsImplications.pdf (Accessed September 2021).

12. This is an adaption of David Harvey. *The new imperialism* (New York: Oxford University Press, 2005).
13. Lucia Michelutti and Barbara Harris-White. *The wild east: criminal political economies in South Asia* (London: UCL Press, 2019) pp. 7–8.
14. Legal exceptionalism was, in fact, the norm in the 'frontier' regions of the Empire, the Pashtun and Baloch formations in northwestern India most of all. See Elizabeth Kolsky (2015) 'The colonial rule of law and the legal regime of exception: frontier "fanaticism" and state violence in British India'. *The American Historical Review* 120 (4) pp. 1218–1246.
15. For a classic, albeit dated theoretical account of 'peripheral capitalism', see Hamza Alavi. 'The structure of peripheral capitalism'. In Hamza Alavi and Teodor Shanin (eds). *Introduction to the sociology of 'developing societies'* (London: Palgrave, 1982) pp. 172–192. Jairus Banaji's inimitable oeuvre is also must-read, especially Jairus Banaji. *Theory as history: Essays on modes of production and exploitation* (Leiden: Brill, 2010). It also worth noting that 'global histories' of capitalism have proliferated in recent years; on the global cotton trade, see Sven Beckert. *Empire of cotton: A global history* (New York: Vintage, 2015). For a distinctly postcolonial perspective, see Andrew B. Liu. *Tea war: A history of capitalism in China and India* (New Haven: Yale University Press, 2020).
16. See Majed Akhter (2015) 'Infrastructure nation: State space, hegemony, and hydraulic regionalism in Pakistan'. *Antipode 47* (4) pp. 849–870. Importantly, what became the agrarian heartland was inhabited previously by pastoral tribes. The very notion of an individual peasant proprietor, then, was as much an invented tradition as in any other part of the colony. Indigenous peoples that that did not conform to the ideal-type 'peasant' mandated by the state-capital dialectic were criminalised, even reified as a 'dangerous class/caste'. See Andrew J. Major (1999) 'State and criminal tribes in colonial Punjab: Surveillance, control and reclamation of the "dangerous classes"'. *Modern Asian Studies* 33 (3) pp. 657–688.
17. See Sharukh Rafi Khan and Aasim Sajjad Akhtar. *The military and denied development in the Pakistani Punjab: An eroding social consensus* (London: Anthem Press, 2014). It is important to note, however, that that colonial Punjab was not a monolith. Revolutionary internationalism, particularly rooted in the Sikh peasant castes, was a significant feature of Punjab's political landscape in the decades before the end of colonial rule. The out-migrations of Sikhs (and Hindus) during and after the partition of Punjab in 1947 had a major stultifying effect on left politics, whilst bolstering

statist hegemony in what remained of Punjab on the Pakistani side of the new border. For a brilliant exposition of Punjab's revolutionary movement in the lead up to and immediate aftermath of India's partition, see Ali Raza. *Revolutionary pasts: communist internationalism in colonial India* (Cambridge: Cambridge University Press, 2020).

18. Shah Mahmoud Hanafi. *Connecting histories in Afghanistan: Market relations and state formation on a colonial frontier* (Stanford: Stanford University Press, 2011).
19. Arif Hasan and Monsoor Raza. *Migration and small towns in Pakistan* (Karachi: Oxford University Press, 2011).
20. Even as Pashtuns and other ethnic groups graduated into a growing intermediate classes with significant presence in expanding urban centres, the same military establishment which facilitated illicit circuits of capital refused to accommodate growing demands for democratisation in the historic peripheral zones. Numerous contradictions were generated by this wilful refusal of state – and Empire – to recognise that the frontier 'tribes' were hardly frozen in time.
21. Ikramul Haq (1996) 'Pak-Afghan drug trade in historical perspective'. *Asian Survey* 36 (10) pp. 945–963.
22. See Nausheen H. Anwar (2016) 'Asian mobilities and state governance at the geographic margins: Geopolitics and oil tales from Karachi to Taftan'. *Environment and Planning A: Economy and Space 48* (6) pp. 1047–1063. The smuggling of contraband as well as human labour to and from the Iranian border is a harrowing endeavour across dirt roads and the perils of organised banditry. Border closings have, in recent times, led to highly publicised deaths as drivers and cargo alike are left to wait without food and water for days on end. See Muhammad Akbar Notezai (2021) 'Starvation awaits drivers along Pak-Iran border'. *DAWN*. 21 April. www.dawn.com/news/1619454/situationer-starvation-awaits-drivers-working-along-pak-iran-border; Muhammad Akbar Notezai (2021) 'On the human smuggling trail'. *DAWN*. 30 May www.dawn.com/news/1626494/on-the-human-smuggling-trail (Accessed September 2021).
23. See Raza Khan (2012) 'Minerals development in FATA'. *FATA Research Centre*. 15 June. https://frc.org.pk/articles/miderals-development-in-fata/ (Accessed September 2021).
24. Mohammad A. Qadeer (2000) 'Ruralopolises: the spatial organisation and residential land economy of high-density rural regions in South Asia'. *Urban Studies 37* (9) pp. 1583–1603. See also Shubra Gururani and Rajarshi Dasgupta (2018) 'Frontier urbanism: Urban-

isation beyond cities in South Asia'. *Economic and Political Weekly* 53 (12) pp. 41–45.

25. In contemporary Pakistan, the manufacturing sector contributes approximately 20% of GDP. Agro-processing industries constitute more than 60% of the sector, both small and big producers connected to global supply chains directly or otherwise. For a useful three-tiered typology of producers that structures the textiles industry and its connections to global supply chains, see Khalida Ghaus, Manzoor H. Memon and Muhammad Asif Iqbal (2017) 'Trade and compliance of labour standards in global supply chains'. *Friedrich Ebert Stiftung.* https://library.fes.de/pdf-files/bueros/pakistan/13953.pdf (Accessed September 2021).
26. For a deep dive into the structure of power in Pakistan's biggest city Karachi, see Laurent Gayer. *Karachi: Ordered disorder and the struggle for the city* (Oxford: Oxford University Press, 2014).
27. Jan Breman's seminal work focused on the Indian state of Gujrat, which was also that country's trend setting neoliberal destination under Chief Minister Narendra Modi in the early 2000s. See Jan Breman. *Footloose labour: Working in India's informal economy* (Cambridge: Cambridge University Press, 1996).
28. Frantz Fanon. *Black skin, white masks* (New York: Grove Press, 1967) p. 18.
29. Lucia Michelutti, Ashraf Hoque, Nicholas Martin, David Picherit, Paul Rollier, Arild E. Ruud and Clarinda Still. *Mafia Raj: The rule of bosses in South Asia* (Stanford: Stanford University Press, 2019) p. 8.
30. Michael Levien. *Dispossession without development: Land grabs in neoliberal India* (Delhi: Oxford University Press, 2018) p. 9.
31. For a succinct summary of the various debates around the concept of accumulation by dispossession, see Derek Hall (2013) 'Primitive accumulation, accumulation by dispossession and the global land grab'. *Third World Quarterly 34* (9) pp. 1582–1604. See also Sam Moyo, Paris Yeros and Praveen Jha (2012) 'Imperialism and primitive accumulation: notes of the new scramble for Africa'. *Agrarian South: Journal of Political Economy 1* (2) pp. 181–203. Finally, Nikita Sud's rich empirical studies of the 'Gujrat model' of development illuminate broader processes of land grabs, dispossession and authoritarian politics in contemporary South Asia. See Nikita Sud (2009) 'The Indian state in a liberalizing landscape'. *Development and Change 40* (4) pp. 645–665; Nikita Sud (2020a) 'Making the political, and doing politics: Unfixed land in an Amoebal Zone in India'. *The Journal of Peasant Studies 47* (6) pp. 1348–1370; Nikita Sud (2020b) 'The actual Gujarat model: Authoritarianism, capitalism, Hindu nation-

alism and populism in the time of Modi'. *Journal of Contemporary Asia*. doi: 10.1080/00472336.2020.1846205

32. A fascinating recent study of the 'state-led moral project' of electrification in post-colonial Asia has coined the term 'fossil developmentalism'. See Elizabeth Chatterjee (2020) 'The Asian anthropocene: Electricity and fossil developmentalism'. *The Journal of Asian Studies* 79 (1) pp. 3–24.
33. By his own admission, Levien's case study is that of a 'successful' example of accumulation by dispossession, by which he means that most of the farmers agreed to leave their lands. As I demonstrate, many forms of dispossession are far from voluntary. While compensation is often a pipe dream, simply surviving the violent wrath of the state and subcontracted goons is no mean feat.
34. '[U]nlike the older developmental state that expropriated large amounts of rural land for public infrastructure and heavy industries, land brokering in the neoliberal era – culminating with SEZs – proceeds under an expansive definition of "public purpose" that is indistinguishable from private capital accumulation. Elite housing colonies, IT parks, malls and amusement parks have joined the hydroelectric dam and steel mill as causes for expropriating the peasantry'. See Michael Levien (2012) 'The land question: special economic zones and the political economy of dispossession in India'. *The Journal of Peasant Studies* 39 (3–4) p. 964.
35. Elizabeth Chatterjee (2020) 'New developmentalism and its discontents: State activism in Modi's Gujarat and India'. *Development and Change*. doi: 10.1111/dech.12579 (Accessed September 2021).
36. Nausheen H. Anwar (2018) 'Receding rurality, booming periphery: Value struggles in Karachi's agrarian-urban frontier'. *Economic & Political Weekly* 53 (12) p. 49.
37. '[A]long the African urban coastal corridor, millions of poor people dream of a four concrete-walled house with sheet metal as a roof. Several other million inhabitants from the middle class wish to benefit from affordable housing programs. Finally, in Accra and Lagos, thousands of wealthy people clamour for luxurious gated communities and shopping malls (in Lagos alone there are over 12,000 millionaires)'. Armelle Choplin (2020) 'Cementing Africa: cement flows and city-making along the West African corridor (Accra, Lomé, Cotonou, Lagos)'. *Urban Studies* 57 (9) p. 1981.
38. Samuel Stein. *Capital city: Gentrification and the real estate state* (New York and London: Verso Books, 2019).

39. Charlotte Lemanski and Sophie Oldfield (2009) 'The parallel claims of gated communities and land invasions in a Southern city: polarised state responses'. *Environment and Planning A 41* (3) p. 634.
40. Long before CPEC, Balochistan's unmatched mineral resources have been fair game for Pakistani subcontractors and global capital. Massive deposits of gold and copper worth up to US$2 trillion at Reko Diq and Saindak in the western district of Chaghai, have been pillaged for over two decades by Chinese, Australian and Chilean multinational companies. Dubious contractual commitments made by the Pakistani government initially translated into windfall profits for the nexus of state and capital. This was soon followed by litigation and a plethora of fines levied against the Pakistani government. The ecological fallouts of the projects, not to mention the almost complete lack of benefits accruing to local populations, have hardly been interrogated. For details about the Reko Diq case, see Amber Darr (2019) 'The Reko Diq "fiasco" in perspective of Pakistan's experience of international investment arbitration'. *London School of Economics and Political Science*. https://blogs.lse.ac.uk/southasia/2019/08/14/long-read-the-reko-diq-fiasco-in-perspective-pakistans-experience-of-international-investment-arbitration (Accessed September 2021).
41. Government ministers have explicitly acknowledged that only 9% of revenues from Gwadar port will accrue to Pakistan. See Iftikhar A. Khan (2017) 'China to get 91pc Gwadar income, minister tells Senate'. *DAWN*. 25 November. www.dawn.com/news/1372695 (Accessed September 2021).
42. Due to constraints of time and space, I am unable to undertake a detailed exposition of the Baloch national question here. Incisive analyses in this regard include Salman R. Sheikh. *The Genesis of Baloch Nationalism: Politics and Ethnicity in Pakistan, 1947–1977* (Oxford: Routledge, 2018); Farhan H. Siddiqui. *The politics of ethnicity in Pakistan: the Baloch, Sindhi and Mohajir ethnic movements* (Oxford: Routledge, 2012); Yunus M. Samad (2014) 'Understanding the insurgency in Balochistan. *Commonwealth & Comparative Politics* 52 (2) pp. 293–320; Alia Amirali. *Balochistan: A case study of Pakistan's peacemaking praxis* (New Dehli: Sage Publications, 2015).
43. The state's planned 'development' of two small islands off the coast of Sindh has also been accompanied by rhetoric about a world class city in the mold of Dubai. See No name (2020) 'Bundal Island will eclipse Dubai with $50 billion investment'.

Express Tribune. 8 October. https://tribune.com.pk/story/2267528/bundal-island-will-eclipse-dubai-with-50-billion-investment

44. See Behram Baloch (2021) 'Gwadar fishermen hold rally against grant of fishing rights to Chinese trawlers'. *DAWN*. 16 June. www.dawn.com/news/1629558 (Accessed September 2021).
45. See Shahmeer Baloch (2021) 'Protests in Pakistan erupt against China's Belt and Road Plan'. *The Guardian* 20 August. www.theguardian.com/environment/2021/aug/20/water-protests-in-pakistan-erupt-against-chinas-belt-and-road-plan (Accessed September 2021).
46. See Maqbool Ahmed (2017) 'Unreal estate: The boom in Gwadar's property market'. *Herald*. June. Intriguingly, the Balochistan High Court ruled in March 2021 that all 'unsettled' land in the province – estimated to be almost 90% of total land – belongs to indigenous tribes. Yet the fate of Gwadar's indigenous population since the construction of the deep sea port began suggests that, even where formal law can ostensibly be mobilised in their favour, *de facto* arrangements in favour of the rich and powerful almost always prevail. See Hasnaat Malik (2021) 'Landmark judgment: "unsettled land" belongs to local tribes: BHC'. *The Express Tribune*. 24 March. https://tribune.com.pk/story/2291055/landmark-judgment-unsettled-land-belongs-to-local-tribes-bhc (Accessed September 2021).
47. Hafeez Jamali (2014) 'A harbor in the tempest: megaprojects, identity, and the politics of place in Gwadar, Pakistan'. Doctoral dissertation: University of Texas-Austin.
48. Maqbool Ahmed (2018) 'The mysterious case of land acquisitions in Balochistan'. *Herald* September.
49. No name (2020) 'Gwadar fencing project kick-starts to make port city safe and secure'. *The Daily Times*. 17 December. https://dailytimes.com.pk/702622/gwadar-fencing-project-kick-starts-to-make-port-city-safe-and-secure (Accessed September 2021).
50. Anwar, 2018.
51. It is worth noting here that all land transfers were in any case undertaken through application of a colonial statute that harkens back to British rule, the Colonisation of Government Land Act of 1912. Another colonial statute, the Land Acquisition Act of 1894, is also regularly invoked to 'legalise' land grabs.
52. See Ishaq Tanoli (2020) 'All construction activities in Bahria Town Karachi are illegal, SCBA tells SHC'. *DAWN*. 22 July. www.dawn.com/news/1570355/all-construction-activities-in-bahria-town-karachi-are-illegal-sbca-tells-shc (Accessed September 2021).

53. See Naziha Syed Ali (2020) 'Malik Riaz and the art of the deal'. *DAWN*. 18 April. https://dawn.com/news/1618221/malik-riaz-the-art-of-the-deal (Accessed September 2021).
54. This resistance has taken place under the guise of the Indigenous Rights Alliance, a loose umbrella outfit of local peoples and progressives committed to protecting the homes, livelihoods and culture of local communities.
55. Levien, 2012, pp. 59–60.
56. Arif Hasan, Noman Ahmed, Mansoor Raza, Asiya Sadiq, Saeed Uddin Ahmed and Moizza B. Sarwar. *Karachi: the land issue* (Karachi: Oxford University Press, 2015) p. 16.
57. Ateeb Ahmed (2021) 'Disciplinary urbanism'. Unpublished manuscript: Department of Geography, Environment and Society, University of Minnesota.
58. Ibid., p. 1.
59. Ibid., p. 6.
60. Adom Getachew. *Worldmaking after empire* (Princeton: Princeton University Press, 2019) p. 17.
61. Juan Gabriel Valdés. *Pinochet's economists: The Chicago school of economics in Chile* (Cambridge: Cambridge University Press, 1995).
62. A *longue duree* analysis of Pakistan's political economy confirms that the state has always played a central role in shaping growth and development, 'state-business relations' consistently and significantly impacting economic outcomes. See Matthew McCartney. *Pakistan-The political economy of growth, stagnation and the state, 1951–2009* (Oxfordshire: Routledge, 2011) p. xviii.
63. S. Akbar Zaidi. *Issues in Pakistan's economy* (Karachi: Oxford University Press, 2015) p. 137.
64. Ayesha Siddiqa. *Military Inc.: inside Pakistan's military economy* (London: Pluto Press, 2007).
65. Hasan H. Karrar and Till Mostowlansky (2020) 'The Belt and Road as political technology: Power and economy in Pakistan and Tajikistan'. *Environment and Planning C: Politics and Space 38* (5) pp. 834–839.
66. Zhaohua Wang, Zahoor Ahmed, Bin Zhang and Bo Wang (2019) 'The nexus between urbanization, road infrastructure, and transport energy demand: empirical evidence from Pakistan'. *Environmental Science and Pollution Research* 26 (34) p. 34889.
67. For some examples of 'development' in the Siraiki belt of South Punjab, see No name (2006) 'Displaced people hold demonstration: WB-funded project' *DAWN*. 9 May. www.dawn.com/news/191411/displaced-people-hold-demonstration-wb-funded-project; No name

(2009) 'Protest against land allotment in Kot Addu' *DAWN*. 28 June. www.dawn.com/news/474269/newspaper/newspaper/column

68. See Aasim Sajjad Akhtar (2018) 'The China Pakistan Economic Corridor: Beyond the rule of capital?'. *Monthly Review 70* (2) pp. 34–48. Chinese president Xi Jinping's announcement in September 2021 that China would no longer finance overseas coal extraction is certainly welcome, but it is unclear whether ongoing CPEC projects will be discontinued. In any case, there is little evidence to suggest that Pakistan's tryst with 'dirty fuel' will end soon. See Zofeen T. Ebrahim (2021) 'China's coal exit will not end Pakistan's reliance on dirty fuel'. *DAWN*. 27 October. www.dawn.com/news/1654355
69. Mustafa Ahmed Khan (2020) 'Making them look the other way! The (ir)rationality of road building in the sindh borderlands of Pakistan'. Unpublished PhD thesis, School of Oriental and African Studies.
70. Ibid., p. 110.
71. A number of activists were threatened by both SECMC goons and the local authorities, and in August 2017 some were even forcibly disappeared by the military's intelligence apparatus, a practice that has become endemic in Pakistan since the onset of the 'war on terror'.
72. Khan, 2020, p. 145.
73. Nosheen Ali. *Delusional States* (Cambridge: Cambridge University Press, 2019) p. 196.
74. Hasan H. Karrar (2020) 'Caravan Trade to Neoliberal Spaces: Fifty years of Pakistan-China connectivity across the Karakoram Mountains'. *Modern Asian Studies*, p. 4. doi: 10.1017/S0026749X20000050
75. Karrar and Mostowlansky, 2020, p. 70.
76. More generally, road-building, construction and other infrastructural interventions are exacerbating longer-term climate change effects in mountain ecology. Ironically, 'almost 40 per cent of the territory has been declared as some form of conservation enclosure, most of which seek to commodify nature for global use and exchange value at the cost of local sovereignty and livelihood'. See Ali, 2019, p. 227.
77. Karrar, 2020, pp. 23–24.
78. Nosheen Ali. 'Grounding Militarism: Structures of Feeling and Force in Gilgit-Baltistan'. In Kamala Visweswaran (ed) *Everyday occupations: experiencing militarism in South Asia and the Middle East* (Philadelphia: University of Pennsylvania Press, 2013) p. 114.

79. Ahmed Rafay Alam, Ali Usman Qasmi, Fizzah Sajjad, Tabitha Spence, Umair Javed and Ammar Ali Jan (2021) 'Remaking a river: land and profit along the Ravi'. *DAWN*. 13 June. www.dawn.com/news/1629117
80. Ibid. The EIA itself can be found at: https://epd.punjab.gov.pk/eia_reports
81. See www.iqair.com/pakistan/punjab/lahore
82. Karl Marx. *Capital: Volume 3* (London: Penguin, 1992).

2 FEAR AND DESIRE

1. I take inspiration here from Kipfer who 'follows Gramsci and treats city and countryside … as intellectual and linguistic-metaphorical claims to hegemony'. See Stefan Kipfer. 'City, country, hegemony: Antonio Gramsci's spatial historicism'. In Michael Ekers, Gillian Hart, Stefan Kipfer and Alex Loftus, (eds) *Gramsci: Space, nature, politics* (New York: John Wiley & Sons, 2012) p. 96.
2. This is particularly true of the prototypical young migrant worker from the 'country' whose parents and grandparents were part of the classical peasantry but for whom 'on the one hand, the umbilical cord to the land is not severed; on the other, the land is not sufficient to support the consumption needs of the peasant household, let alone generating additional funds for accumulation of capital. The peasant is forced to work in the non-farming unorganized sector, or as an informal labourer in the organized sector. But unlike the push factor–led migration of traditional development economics, such migration is transitory. What is permanent is the ceaseless circulation of a footloose labour force across the subcontinent in tandem with the farming cycles'. See Deepankar Basu and Debarshi Das (2013) 'The Maoist movement in India: Some political economy considerations'. *Journal of Agrarian Change 13* (3) p. 376.
3. The BJP under Narendra Modi is certainly the obvious parallel to the PTI under Imran Khan, but I find it more useful to trace the origins of motifs like 'corruption' and 'rule of law' that have undergirded the emergence of such leaders/parties in the current conjuncture. In India's case, Anna Hazare's anti-corruption movement was crucial in mobilising 'middle-class' public opinion at large. This movement directly resulted in the formation and electoral success in the Delhi capital area of the Aam Admi Party (AAM) led by Arwind Kerjiwal. For incisive and critical takes on AAM, see Aheli Chowdhury (2019) 'Anti-corruption movement: A story of the making of the Aam Admi Party and the interplay of political representation in India'. *Politics*

and Governance 7 (3) pp. 189–198; Stephanie Tawa Lama-Rewal (2019) 'Political representation in the discourse and practices of the "party of the common man" in India'. *Politics and Governance* 7 (3) pp. 179–188.

4. Imran Khan. *Pakistan: A personal history* (New York: Random House, 2011) pp. 149–150.
5. Tabinda Khan. 'Pakistan Tehreek-e-Insaaf: From movement to a catch-all party'. In Mariam Mufti, Sahar Shafqat and Niloufer Siddiqui (eds). *Pakistan's political parties: Surviving between dictatorship and democracy* (Washington DC: Georgetown University Press, 2020) p. 67.
6. Nor was it considered ready by the omnipotent military establishment to be given the reins of government. By 2018, however, the PTI and Imran Khan were catapulted to power through a mixture of pre and post poll rigging. See Aqil Shah (2019a) 'Pakistan in 2018: Theft of an election'. *Asian Survey* 59 (1) pp. 98–107.
7. Haroon K. Ullah. *Vying for Allah's vote: Understanding Islamic parties, political violence and extremism in Pakistan* (Washington DC: Georgetown University Press, 2014) pp. 150–153.
8. Importantly, dozens if not hundreds of ANP activists and leaders were killed both while the party ran the KP provincial government (2008–2013) and afterwards. On the face of it attacks were perpetrated by right-wing militants, but the prevailing feeling within the ANP and amongst critical observers more generally is that the state's own security apparatus was at the very least complicit in the wilful targeting of the party.
9. Umair Javed (2019) 'Continuity and change in Naya Pakistan'. *Catalyst* 2 (4) pp. 98–99.
10. Giorgio Agamben. *State of exception* (Chicago: University of Chicago Press, 2005) p. 87.
11. For an incisive and impassioned analysis of the Indian 'state of exception', see Ananya Vajpeyi. *Prolegomena to the study of people and places in violent India* (Delhi: WISCOMP Foundation for Universal Responsibility, 2007).
12. '[R]epressive social control and containment strategies, including a vicious criminalization of the marginalized, often racialized and ethnicized, and the mobilization of the "culture industries", dehumanize the victims of global capitalism as dangerous, depraved, and culturally degenerate Others, as criminal elements posing a threat to society. At the same time, the culture of global capitalism attempts to seduce the excluded and abandoned into petty consumption and fantasy as an alternative to placing social or political demands on the

system through mobilization'. See William I. Robinson. *Global capitalism and the crisis of humanity* (Cambridge: Cambridge University Press, 2014) p. 95–96.

13. For an insightful commentary of Tocqueville's contradictions and how to read them in our present, see Lina Benabdallah (2020) 'On Tocqueville in Algeria and epistemic violence'. *Al-Jazeera English.* www.aljazeera.com/indepth/opinion/tocqueville-algeria-epistemic-violence-200706122518091.html.
14. Max Pensky. 'Radical critique and late epistemology: Tocqueville, Adorno and authoritarianism'. In Wendy Brown, Peter E. Gordon and Max Pensky. *Authoritarianism: Three inquiries in critical theory* (Chicago: University of Chicago Press, 2018) p. 101.
15. For an insightful articulation of the perils of detaching the politics of race from class, see Asad Haider. *Mistaken identity: race and class in the age of Trump* (New York and London: Verso, 2018).
16. Goran Therborn (2020) 'Dreams and nightmares of the world's middle classes'. *New Left Review* 124 July–August pp. 63–87.
17. Andrew Wilder. *The Pakistani voter, electoral politics and voting behaviour in the Punjab* (Karachi: Oxford University Press, 1999).
18. In previous work I have suggested that the 'high bureaucracy' of the state ceased to be the preserve of urbane, Anglicised elements from the 1980s onwards. In a recent essay, Saeed Shafqat makes the intriguing point that, under the regime of neoliberal globalisation, a foreign educated class of young professionals that he terms the 'laptop wallahs' are once again interested in employment in the public sector. See Saeed Shafqat. 'Praetorians and the people' in Maleeha Lodhi (ed) *Pakistan: Beyond the crisis state* (Karachi: Oxford University Press, 2011) pp. 95–112.
19. S. Akbar Zaidi. *Issues in Pakistan's economy* (Karachi: Oxford University Press, 2015) pp. 5178–5180.
20. Generally speaking, 'honour killings' refer to vengeful murder of young women and men who have defied their families in their choice of partner, which, if consummated in legal form, are often called 'love marriages'. These choices often transgress boundaries of caste, religion, *biraderi* (patrilineal lineage) and other such entrenched social divides.
21. Dibyesh Anand (2012) 'China and India: Postcolonial informal empires in the emerging global order'. *Rethinking Marxism 24* (1) p. 69.
22. See Rahi Gaikwad (2009) 'Manmohan: naxalism the greatest internal threat'. *The Hindu.* www.thehindu.com/news/national/Manmohan-naxalism-the-greatest-internal-threat/article16886121.ece

23. Rosa Luxemburg. *The accumulation of capital* (Abingdon and New York: Routledge, 2003) p. 594.
24. Alpa Shah. *Nightmarch: Among India's revolutionary guerrillas* (Chicago: University of Chicago Press, 2019).
25. Soon after partition, Nehru-led Congress government made clear that it would not tolerate left militancy under any guise, crushing the communist-led Telengana Peasant Revolt in the ex-princely state of Hyderabad Deccan. This made clear that parliamentary communism was the only form of left politics acceptable to the postcolonial Indian state. See John Roosa (2001) 'Passive revolution meets peasant revolution: Indian nationalism and the Telangana revolt'. *The Journal of Peasant Studies 28* (4) pp. 57–94.
26. Kapil S. Komireddi. *Malevolent republic: A short history of the new India* (Delhi, Oxford University Press, 2019).
27. In May 2018, all the Pashtun areas on the border with Afghanistan – formerly known as FATA – were formally merged into the Khyber Pakhtunkhwa province, colonial-era legal exceptionalism finally giving way to formal citizenship. The actual practice of the everyday state, however, remains to date largely unchanged, with military presence and punitive state logics particularly notable.
28. Maria Rashid has recently expanded the debate over military dominance in Pakistan to the realm of 'affect'. On the basis of fieldwork in the Punjabi district of Chakwal, she documents the meticulously choreographing of 'sacrifice' of soldiers killed in combat. While soldiers' families – mothers, sisters and wives in particular – are called upon to publicly grieve and celebrate alike, an otherwise hegemonic field is riven by ambivalences. See Maria Rashid. *Dying to serve: Militarism, affect, and the politics of sacrifice in the Pakistan army* (Stanford: Stanford University Press, 2020).
29. Yunus Samad. *The Pakistan-US conundrum: Jihadists, the military and the people-the struggle for control* (London: Hurst Publishers, 2011).
30. It is far more useful, I think, to situate the global 'war on terror' within the broader rubric of 'humanitarian imperialism' that was inaugurated following the end of the Cold War to coincide with the unleashing of capital to all corners of the globe. See Ray Kiely. *Rethinking imperialism* (London: Macmillan International, 2001).
31. Civilian populations in urban centres in Pakistan did indeed experience an increase in violent attacks during the 2000s and early 2010, the metropolitan areas of Karachi, Islamabad, Quetta, Peshawar and Lahore targeted most conspicuously. For official figures, see https://nacta.gov.pk/terrorism-decline-in-pakistan/

32. For a critical analysis of the impact of US military aid to Pakistan, both during the 'war on terror' and previously, see S. Akbar Zaidi (2011) 'Who benefits from US aid to Pakistan?'. *Economic and Political Weekly XLVI* (32) pp. 103–109.
33. Even as war-ravaged Pashtuns suffered brutalisation – in their ancestral villages and metropoles alike – Pakistan's most historically exploited and brutalised periphery Balochistan was experiencing a nationalist insurgency of its own. Aptly described as Pakistan's 'secret dirty war' because of its much more sporadic place in the mediatised public's imaginary, military actions against Baloch insurgents in the south-west of the country began as early as 2004 and continue to this day. See Declan Walsh (2011) 'Pakistan's secret dirt war'. *The Guardian* 29 March.
34. Aasim Sajjad Akhtar (2010) 'Islam as ideology of tradition and change: The "new jihad" in swat, Northern Pakistan'. *Comparative studies of South Asia, Africa and the Middle East 30* (3) pp. 595–609.
35. Humeira Iqtidar (2009) 'Who are the Taliban in Swat?'. *OpenDemocracy*. www.opendemocracy.net/en/who-are-the-taliban-in-swat/
36. Saadia Toor (2012) 'Imperialist feminism redux'. *Dialectical Anthropology 36* (3) pp. 147–160.
37. Pamir Halimzai Sahill (2018) 'The terror speaks: Inside Pakistan's terrorism discourse and national action plan'. *Studies in Conflict & Terrorism 41* (4) pp. 319–337.
38. I met many refugees from Swat in temporary camps in Mardan district in the immediate aftermath of the 2009 operation, and continued to maintain contact with them in subsequent years; some returned to Swat while others relocated permanently in cities like Islamabad and Karachi. For an insightful rendition of the intimate suffering and coping mechanisms of the displaced Pashtun 'refugee' in urban Pakistan, see Ammara Maqsood (2019) 'The social life of rumors: Uncertainty in everyday encounters between the military, Taliban, and tribal Pashtun in Pakistan'. *Comparative Studies of South Asia, Africa and the Middle East 39* (3) pp. 462–474.
39. For an extremely rich empirical as well as sophisticated theoretical treatise on the ebbs and flows of class, ethnic-national identity, gender and other determinants of Karachi's politics, see Ayyaz Mallick (2020) 'The (un)making of the working class in Karachi, 1980s-2010s'. PhD Thesis York University, Toronto.
40. Sahill, 2018, p. 10.
41. The case of neoliberal Istanbul under Erdogan's AKP in the early 2010s offers an interesting comparison. 'Istanbul's real-estate boom in the early 2010s was due to a series of legal and policy changes that

facilitated lucrative urban transformation projects at the expense of the systematic displacement and dispossession of urban poor and middle classes in the mega city. While the AKP received international support as a good business facilitator, its success story masked the violence of forceful evictions, the displacement of the working class away from working class jobs, the lack of democratic governance, aggressive gentrification, rent unfriendly policies, and the destruction of cultural heritage embedded in the party's urban policy, along with the massive wealth transfer this policy triggered through state-led real-estate creation and speculation'. See Sinan Erensü and Ayca Alemdaroğlu (2018) 'Dialectics of reform and repression: Unpacking Turkey's authoritarian "turn"'. *Review of Middle East Studies* 52 (1) p. 24.

42. For a detailed exposition of the I-11 demolition, see Aasim Sajjad Akhtar and Ammar Rashid (2021) 'Dispossession and the militarised developer state: Financialisation and class power on the agrarian–urban frontier of Islamabad, Pakistan'. *Third World Quarterly*. doi: 10.1080/01436597.2021.1939004
43. Mike Davis. *Planet of slums* (New York and London: Verso, 2006) p. 17.
44. Aasim Sajjad Akhtar (2018) 'The China Pakistan Economic Corridor: Beyond the rule of capital?'. *Monthly Review* 70 (2) pp. 34–48.
45. See No name (2015) 'Operation to demolish Afghan Basti launched in Islamabad'. *Dunyanews*. https://dunyanews.tv/en/Pakistan/291087-Operation-to-demolish-Afghan-Basti-launched-in-Isl
46. Focusing on the case of the renowned Okara peasant movement in central Punjab, Rizvi elucidates how anti-terrorist legislation has been employed to criminalise resistance to 'development': '[T]he state can choose to surveil, engage and control select populations like peasant farmers through the idiom of counterterrorism, if not development. Conversely, the security state, its expropriation of land or its infrastructural projects are cloaked in secrecy and exceptionalism'. See Mubashir Rizvi (2018) 'From terrorism to dispossession: Pakistan's Anti-Terrorism Act as a means of eviction'. *Anthropology Today* 34 (3) p. 18.
47. Slums and squatter settlements are often found in close proximity to 'middle-class' homeowners in big cities – it is common practice for the latter to regularly complain to local authorities about slum residents' conduct, and, when enough of a 'consensus' is forged in and around 'anti-encroachment' operations, to demand that the settlement in their neighbourhood be demolished.

48. 'If the decentralization and dispersal around the world of manufacturing processes represented the leading edge of an earlier wave of globalization, the current wave involves the decentralization and global dispersal of services. Data processing, insurance claims, phone operators, call centers, software production, marketing, journalism and publishing, health and telemedicine, medical and legal transcriptions, advertising, banking – these and many other services are now undertaken through complex webs of outsourcing, subcontracting, and transnational alliances among firms'. See Robinson, 2014, p. 25.
49. Available at https://cdn.techjuice.pk/wp-content/uploads/2019/08/Index-freelance.pdf
50. Christian Fuchs (2016) 'Digital labor and imperialism'. *Monthly Review* 67 (8) p. 14.
51. See Brenna Bhandar and Rafeef Ziadah. *Revolutionary feminisms: Conversations on collective action and radical thought* (London: Verso, 2020) p. 157.
52. Careem was formally launched in Pakistan in 2016, later acquired by Uber in early 2019.
53. Fleeting protests organised by 'Captains' against changing contractual terms between themselves and the company have amounted to little. See www.dawn.com/news/1520144
54. Take, for instance, the CEO of Careem outlining his vision in April 2017 for the company to 'create one million job opportunities by 2020 and attract US$10bn of investment in public transport infrastructure'. See https://aurora.dawn.com/news/1141986. Speaking on the condition of anonymity, a Careem employee in early 2020 told me that such rosy figures are part of a public relations strategy that bears little resemblance to actual targets.
55. Dina M. Siddiqi (2015) 'Starving for justice: Bangladeshi garment workers in a "post-Rana plaza" world'. *International Labor and Working-Class History* (87) pp. 165–173; S. A. Shumi, M. H. Zuidgeest, J. A. Martinez, D. Efroymson and M. F. van Maarseveen (2015) 'Understanding the relationship between walkability and quality-of-life of women garment workers in Dhaka, Bangladesh'. *Applied Research in Quality Of Life* 10 (2) pp. 263–287.
56. In many cases, women working in agriculture as well as non-farm rural sectors do not earn anything at all due to various forms of indenture; in smallholding peasant families, women's unpaid labour typically contributes to household production.
57. Zofeen Ebrahim (2020) 'Pakistan's younger women riding a digital wave in drive for better jobs'. *Reuters*. 28 April. www.reuters.com/

article/pakistan-women-technology-idUKL5N2CD08B (Accessed September 2021).

58. Aimen Siddiqui (2019) 'Fast and professional: Women behind the wheel'. *The News International*. 8 March.
59. Nancy Fraser, Tithi Bhattacharya and Cinzia Arruzza (2018) 'Notes for a feminist manifesto'. *New Left Review*, 114 p. 113.

3 THE DIGITAL LIFEWORLD

1. These impressions were first penned by Schwab in an article in December 2015 edition of the influential establishment publication *Foreign Affairs*. See www.foreignaffairs.com/articles/2015-12-12/fourth-industrial-revolution. On the left, Therborn contends that we are living through the third industrial revolution, 'after the first of steam and coal, the second of electricity and the combustion engine'. See Goran Therborn (2016) 'An age of progress?'. *New Left Review* 99 p. 27.
2. For a *longue duree* analysis, see Fred Turner. *From counterculture to cyberculture: Stewart Brand, the Whole Earth Network, and the rise of digital utopianism* (Chicago: University of Chicago Press, 2010). For a more molecular understanding of the 'progressive' tendencies that explain recent organisational forms in the software programming sub-sector of Big Tech, see Micheal Eby (2021) 'Agile Workplace' *NLR – Sidecar*. https://newleftreview.org/sidecar/posts/agile-workplace.
3. The shutdown of 'normal' life due to the novel coronavirus in 2020 and the initiation of online classes, for example, was experienced by many educated young people in Pakistan, especially from ethnic peripheries, as highly exclusionary, internet service provision in their native towns and villages simply not sufficient to partake meaningfully. See Mehreen Zahra-Malik (2020) 'The coronavirus effect on Pakistan's digital divide'. *BBC Worklife*. www.bbc.com/worklife/article/20200713-the-coronavirus-effect-on-pakistans-digital-divide.
4. In Pakistan's specific case, a formal 'Digital Pakistan' initiative was launched by the Imran Khan-led PTI government in 2019, headed by a former Chief Executive of Google. See https://digitalpakistan.pk/home.html
5. Based on the Ghanaian case, Bernards makes a compelling argument for the colonial roots of 'financial inclusion'. See Nick Bernards (2021) 'Poverty finance and the durable contradictions of colonial capitalism: Placing "financial inclusion" in the long run in Ghana'. *Geoforum* 123 pp. 89–98.

6. A. A. Kemal (2019) 'Mobile banking in the government-to-person payment sector for financial inclusion in Pakistan'. *Information Technology for Development* 25 (3) pp. 475–502.
7. SPN 365–356 (Q10,1I§12).
8. Nancy Fraser. 'Rethinking the public sphere: A contribution to the critique of actually existing democracy'. In Craig Calhoun (ed) *Habermas and the public sphere* (Cambridge: MIT Press, 1992).
9. Sudipta Kaviraj (1997) 'Filth and the public sphere: Concepts and practices about space in Calcutta'. *Public Culture 10* (1) p. 89.
10. Tan Tai Yong (1995) 'Punjab and the making of Pakistan: The roots of a civil-military state'. *South Asia: Journal of South Asian Studies 18* (1) pp. 177–192.
11. Partha Chatterjee. *Lineages of political society: Studies in postcolonial democracy* (New York: Columbia University Press, 2011).
12. For an incisive demonstration of how 'political society' is in fact a domain that transcends the elite-subaltern binary, see Nicholas Martin (2014) 'The dark side of political society: patronage and the reproduction of social inequality'. *Journal of Agrarian Change 14* (3) pp. 419–434.
13. Stanley Aronowitz (1989) 'Postmodernism and politics'. *Social Text 18* p. 101.
14. Goran Therborn. *From Marxism to post-Marxism* (London and New York: Verso, 2008) p. 18. Reflecting on the specific intellectual trajectories of scholarship on the postcolonial world, Bannerji notes, '[w]e no longer spoke of anti-colonial independence, national liberation or class struggles, but of a cultural colonialism and its afterlife in postcolonialism … Critique of colonialism was thus divorced from that of capitalism and imperialism'. See Brenna Bhandar and Rafeef Ziadah. *Revolutionary feminisms: Conversations on collective action and radical thought* (London: Verso, 2020) pp. 116–117.
15. It is important to note that contemporary progressives in Pakistan have come of age politically and intellectually under the shadow of 'progressive neoliberalism' as well as alarmism vis a vis 'religious extremism'. More generally, they have been exposed to mainstream historical accounts of actually existing socialist regimes during the Cold War in which Leninist party-state models of political organisation are generally derided as undemocratic. All of which has given rise to models of collective action in the current conjuncture in which 'horizontalism' is celebrated and emphasised as representing a genuinely revolutionary imaginary. See John Chalcraft (2012) 'Horizontalism in the Egyptian revolutionary process'. *Middle East Report 262* (42) pp. 6–11.

16. I thank Tooba Syed for alerting me to the significance of these 'lower-class' publics.
17. Payal Arora. *The next billion users* (Cambridge: Harvard University Press, 2019) p. 2.
18. See, for instance, Pankaj Mishra and Viet Thanh Nguyen (2020) '"Free speech has never been freer": Pankaj Mishra and Viet Thanh Nguyen in conversation'. *The Guardian Books.* www.theguardian.com/books/2020/jul/24/free-speech-has-never-been-freer-pankaj-mishra-and-viet-thanh-nguyen-in-conversation
19. Byung-Chul Han, Byung-Chul. *In the swarm: Digital prospects* (Cambridge: MIT Press, 2017).
20. Max Haiven. *Revenge capitalism: The ghosts of empire, the demons of capital, and the settling of unpayable debts* (London: Pluto Press, 2020).
21. Paulo Gerbaudo (2018) 'Social media and populism: an elective affinity?'. *Media, Culture & Society 40* (5) pp. 745–753.
22. Aasim Sajjad Akhtar (2017) 'The Zia generation'. *DAWN*. 21 April. www.dawn.com/news/1328233
23. Abdul Basit (2020) 'Barelvi political activism and religious mobilization in Pakistan: The case of Tehreek-e-Labaik Pakistan (TLP)'. *Politics, Religion & Ideology 21* (3) pp. 374–389.
24. I deploy the umbrella term 'progressive' with caution, primarily in contradistinction from the umbrella term 'reactionary'. In no sense does this term imply a commitment to an uncritical view of 'progress' or 'modernisation' more generally.
25. William Davies (2021) 'The politics of recognition in the age of social media'. *New Left Review 128* p. 96.
26. Tugal argues that much of the 'post-2009 wave' of popular revolt was motivated in significant part by a middle strata, or what he calls the 'new petty bourgeoisie'. Importantly, this strata and its often wildly varying political alignments, must be understood in terms of its 'contradictory class locations'. See Cihan Tugal (2015) 'Elusive revolt: The contradictory rise of middle class politics'. *Thesis Eleven* 130 (1) pp. 74–95.
27. Sara Salem. 'Creating spaces for dissent: The role of social media in the 2011 Egyptian revolution', in Daniel Trottier and Christian Fuchs (eds). *Social media, politics and the state: Protests, revolutions, riots, crime and policing in the age of Facebook, Twitter and YouTube* (Oxford: Routledge, 2014).
28. Jodi Dean. 'Critique or collectivity? Communicative capitalism and the subject of politics'. In David Chandler and Christian Fuchs. *Digital objects, digital subjects: Interdisciplinary perspectives on capi-*

talism, labour and politics in the age of big data (London: University of Westminster Press, 2019) p. 172–173. See also Nick Srnicek. *Platform capitalism* (New York: John Wiley & Sons, 2017).

29. Achin Vanaik (2018) 'India's two hegemonies'. *New Left Review 112* p. 47. Empirical evidence from the 2019 general election suggests that greater numbers of the 'poor' – including oppressed castes – cast their votes for Modi and the BJP than in 2014. See Christophe Jaffrelot (2019) 'Class and caste in the 2019 Indian election–why have so many poor started voting for Modi?'. *Studies in Indian Politics 7* (2) pp. 149–160.
30. See, for example, Dylan Riley (2018) 'What is Trump?' *New Left Review 114*. November–December.
31. At the time of writing, the term 'hybrid regime' has become common currency to describe Imran Khan's government. Coined initially by Cyril Almeida, an English columnist who fell foul of the military establishment under the previous PML-N dispensation (2013–2018), 'hybrid' suggests a regime type whereby civilians (PTI, Imran Khan, etc.) are the face of decision-making while military overlords exercise real power. Notwithstanding the distinctiveness of the 'hybrid regime', however, the military has always exercised considerable influence over all civilian regimes. See, for example Mazhar Aziz. *Military control in Pakistan: The parallel state* (Oxford: Routledge, 2007).
32. Waziristan's principal tribes are the Mehsuds and Wazirs; PTM's primary success derived from its ability to mobilise support across tribal identities.
33. Baqir Sajjad Syed (2018) 'Army-PTM talks stall after promising start'. *DAWN*. 4 May. www.dawn.com/news/1405541
34. A short documentary commissioned by *Al-Jazeera* aptly titled 'War, lies and hashtags' explores both the euphoric and desperate life of a well-known PTI propagandist who is 'digital commander' of a young troll army. www.aljazeera.com/programmes/witness/2020/05/war-lies-hashtags-pakistan-twitter-battles-200512080420931.html
35. See Shiffa Yousafzai (2018) 'From a Yousafzai to Manzoor Pashteen – not in my name!!' *Global Village Space*. 9 May. www.globalvillagespace.com/from-a-yousafzai-to-manzoor-pashteen-not-in-my-name/
36. See No name (2019) 'Gulalai Ismail: Activist in hiding flees Pakistan for the US'. *BBC*. 20 September. www.bbc.co.uk/news/world-asia-49765178
37. See, for instance, www.nbcnews.com/id/41561718/ns/world_news-south_and_central_asia/t/pakistan-army-turns-war-movies-counter-jihad/#.XzqkRuhKhPY; and www.thenews.com.pk/latest/447360-pakistan-day-ispr-releases-new-song

38. www.ispr.gov.pk/press-release-detail.php?id=5385
39. Maria Rashid. *Dying to serve: Militarism, affect, and the politics of sacrifice in the Pakistan army* (Stanford: Stanford University Press, 2020) p. 16.
40. Zulfiqar Ali (2021) 'Waziristan MNA, nationalists form political party'. *DAWN*. 2 September. www.dawn.com/news/1644028
41. Rubina Saigol and Nida U. Chaudhry. *Contradictions and ambiguities of feminism in Pakistan: Exploring the fourth wave* (Islamabad: Friedrich Ebert Stiftung, 2020).
42. Farida Shaheed. 'The women's movement in Pakistan: Challenges and achievements'. In Amrita Basu (ed) *Rethinking global women's movements* (Oxford: Routledge, 2010).
43. Saigol and Chaudhry, 2020, p. 7.
44. Anmol Irfan (2021) 'How a feminist movement in Pakistan keeps growing despite an entrenched patriarchy and continuous media shakedowns'. *Newline Magazine*. 28 April. https://newlinesmag.com/reportage/pakistans-aurat-march-and-its-unrelenting-feminists
45. Bhandar and Ziadah, 2020, p. 114.
46. Tanner Mirrlees (2021) 'Socialists on social media platforms: Communicating within and against digital capitalism'. *Socialist Register 57* pp. 125–126.
47. Ibid., p. 31. The acronym of FAANG is also increasingly common: Facebook, Apple, Amazon, Netflix, Google.
48. Regulatory authorities in Pakistan have also imposed short bans on TikTok, PUBG and other Chinese social media platforms over the years. See No name (2020) 'Pakistan lifts TikTok ban for a second time'. *Al Jazeera*. 1 April. www.aljazeera.com/news/2021/4/1/pakistan-lifts-tiktok-ban-for-a-second-time
49. David Golumbia (2015) 'The amazonization of everything'. *Jacobin*. 5 August.
50. Nick Couldry and Ulises A. Mejias. *The costs of connection: How data are colonizing human life and appropriating it for capitalism* (Stanford: Stanford University Press, 2019).
51. This is underlined by the existence, among others, of a substantial 'digital gender gap'. See https://webfoundation.org/research/costs-of-exclusion-report/

4 THE CLASSLESS SUBJECT

1. Eric Hobsbawm. *The age of extremes: The short twentieth century, 1914–1991* (London: Penguin, 1994) p. 460.

2. For a robust empirical argument that situates the 'endless crisis' in the long-term secular trends of monopoly-finance capitalism, see John Bellamy Foster and Robert W. McChesney. *The endless crisis: How monopoly-finance capital produces stagnation and upheaval from the USA to China* (New York: Monthly Review Press, 2017).
3. For an incisive exploration of a 'new political generation' of millennials who are more educated than their parents but without the same opportunities for mobility, see Ruth Milkman (2017) 'A new political generation: Millennials and the post-2008 wave of protest'. *American Sociological Review* 82 (1) pp. 1–31.
4. This has been proven most conclusively in the case of the British Labour Party, officials of which actively colluded in the opposition to the Corbyn faction in the 2017 general election. See https://cryptome.org/2020/04/Labour-Antisemitism-Report.pdf
5. Nick Srnicek and Alex Williams. *Inventing the future: Postcapitalism and a world without work* (London and New York: Verso Books, 2015) p. 78.
6. Frantz Fanon. *The wretched of the earth* (London: McGibbon and Kee, 1965) p. 246.
7. David Harvey. *The condition of postmodernity* (Oxford: Blackwell, 1990).
8. Nancy Fraser (1995) 'From redistribution to recognition? Dilemmas of justice in a "post-socialist" age'. *New Left Review* 212.
9. Aditya Nigam. *Desire named development* (Delhi: Penguin Books India, 2011).
10. SPN 352; Q10II§54.
11. The idea is articulated further: 'The road is long and, in part, unknown. We recognize our limitations. We will make the human being of the 21st century – we, ourselves. We will forge ourselves in daily action, creating a new man and woman with a new technology'. See Che Guevara and Margarita Zimmermann. *Man and socialism in Cuba* (Havana: Guairas Book Institute, 1967).
12. Marx's famous reflections in *Critique of a Gotha Program* are also relevant: '[A]fter the enslaving subordination of the individual to the division of labor, and therewith also the antithesis between mental and physical labor, has vanished; after labor has become not only a means of life but life's prime want; after the productive forces have also increased with the all-around development of the individual, and all the springs of co-operative wealth flow more abundantly – only then can the narrow horizon of bourgeois right be crossed in its entirety and society inscribe on its banners: From each according to

his ability, to each according to his needs!' Karl Marx. *Critique of the Gotha Program* (New York: International Publishers, 1938) p. 36.

13. Dipesh Chakrabarty. *The climate of history in a planetary age* (Chicago: University of Chicago Press, 2021) p. 103.
14. Ayyaz Mallick (2020) 'From Partisan universal to concrete universal? The Pashtun Tahaffuz movement in Pakistan'. *Antipode* 52 (6) pp. 1774–1793.
15. For a refreshingly clear yet critical take on the complex dialectics of (post) development, difference, capital and representation, see Kiran Asher and Joel Wainwright (2019) 'After post-development: On capitalism, difference, and representation'. *Antipode* 51 (1) pp. 25–44.
16. Brenna Bhandar and Rafeef Ziadah. *Revolutionary feminisms: Conversations on collective action and radical thought* (London: Verso, 2020) p. 111.
17. Fanon, 1965, p. 177.
18. SPN, 9; Q12§3.
19. Chakrabarty, 2021, p. 111.
20. Fanon, 1965, pp. 315–316.
21. Ali Raza. *Revolutionary pasts: communist internationalism in colonial India* (Cambridge: Cambridge University Press, 2020) p. 254.
22. Michael Denning (2021) 'Everyone a legislator'. *New Left Review* 129 p. 43.
23. Umair Javed (2021) 'A decade of change and stagnation'. *DAWN*. 20 September. www.dawn.com/news/1647288/a-decade-of-change-stagnation
24. In a handful of sectors, legislation has been passed to protect workers, but there is to date effectively zero enforcement. The most notable example was a bill to abolish bonded labour, passed by Parliament in 1992. The practice of indenture, and various forms of debt bondage nevertheless remain endemic, especially in brick kilns. A domestic workers union was incorporated for the first time in 2015 with the assistance of donors, betraying a lack of organic roots within workers themselves. See www.ilo.org/islamabad/info/public/pr/WCMS_338484/lang--en/index.htm
25. Qalandar B. Memon (2010) 'Blood on the path of love: The striking workers of Faisalabad, Pakistan'. *Monthly Review* 62 (7); Rina Agarwala. *Informal labor, formal politics, and dignified discontent in India* (Cambridge: Cambridge University Press, 2013).
26. Aasim Sajjad Akhtar (2005) 'Privatisation at gunpoint'. *Monthly Review* 57 (5); Aasim Sajjad Akhtar (2010b) 'The oil and gas brigade: fragmented responses to capitalist penetration in Pakistan's Sindh province'. *Labour, Capital and Society* 43 (1) pp. 6–30.

27. See Aasim Sajjad Akhtar (2011) 'Patronage and class in urban Pakistan: Modes of labor control in the contractor economy'. *Critical Asian Studies* 43 (2) pp. 159–184; Mansoor Raza and Hasan Manzoor (2016) 'On death's door: Trade unions in Pakistan'. *DAWN*. 1 May. www.dawn.com/news/1255333
28. The Gulf migrations from the mid-1970s instigated significant social change in rural Pakistan, but immigration policies in the hitherto accessible Gulf states have become progressively more conservative. Nevertheless, labour continues to be Pakistan's major export, an indicator of demographic pressures as much as any other factor.
29. It is also worth bearing in mind that a large number of 'agriculturalists' in Pakistan rely more on rearing livestock to meet livelihood needs than on farming *per se*, particularly in non-irrigated regions. Furthermore, pastoral communities continue to survive, even though many members tend towards daily wage work in agriculture in the face of attacks on the common grazing lands that sustain them.
30. Sam Moyo, Praveen Jha and Paris Yeros (2013) 'The classical agrarian question: Myth, reality and relevance today'. *Agrarian South: Journal of Political Economy* 2 (1) pp. 93–119; Chris Carlson (2018) 'Rethinking the agrarian question: Agriculture and underdevelopment in the Global South'. *Journal of Agrarian Change* 18 (4) pp. 703–721.
31. The last prominent 'peasant movement' around control/ownership of agricultural land in Pakistan was centred in the Okara district of central Punjab, but its unique characteristics – primarily that the demand for 'land reform' revolved around state-owned farms – were not replicable across Punjab or Pakistan more generally. See Aasim Sajjad Akhtar (2006) 'The state as landlord in Pakistani Punjab: Peasant struggles on the Okara military farms'. *Journal of Peasant Studies* 33 (3) pp. 479–501. For a more critical appraisal of the movement and its various interlocutors, see Mubashir Rizvi. *The ethics of staying: social movements and land rights politics in Pakistan* (Stanford: Stanford University Press, 2019).
32. Indeed, the Indian farmers struggle which brought millions onto the streets in 2020–2021 is an important reminder that dispossession is not necessarily the only instigating factor for peasant politics. Triggered by the Modi government's desire to enact new laws governing the agrarian sector that would increase the power of multinational agribusiness, withdraw state subsidies and contribute to the slow but steady squeeze on small and medium sized family farms, the movement has no parallel in Pakistan. An organ-

isation that goes by the name Kissan Ittehad (Peasant Collective) has mobilised farmers in Punjab province, but more than the small and landless peasantry most of its constituents tend to be affluent farmers who seek concessions from the government rather than substantial reform.

33. Faisal Devji. *Muslim Zion: Pakistan as a political idea* (Cambridge: Harvard University Press, 2013).
34. I referred earlier to some recent works on Pakistan's contemporary ethnic-national movements. Others include Adeel Khan. *Politics of identity: Ethnic nationalism and the state in Pakistan* (Delhi: Sage Publications, 2005); Nukhbah Taj Langah. *Poetry as resistance: Islam and ethnicity in postcolonial Pakistan* (Dehli: Routledge India, 2012).
35. Mallick, 2020, p. 1787.
36. John O' Brien. *The unconquered people: The liberation journey of an oppressed caste* (Karachi: Oxford University Press, 2012).
37. Nancy Fraser (2016) 'Crisis of care'. *New Left Review 100* pp. 1–20.
38. Maria Rashid. *Dying to serve: Militarism, affect, and the politics of sacrifice in the Pakistan army* (Stanford: Stanford University Press, 2020).
39. bell hooks. *Feminism is for everybody: Passionate politics* (London: Pluto Press, 2000).
40. It is also important to note here that sexual abuse against young boys is virtually endemic in many religious schools. See www.trtworld.com/magazine/shhhh-don-t-say-a-word-child-abuse-case-rocks-pakistan-s-clergy-47739
41. Nancy Fraser (2021) 'Climates of capital'. *New Left Review 127* p. 97.
42. Indeed, even more contemporary versions of the left-wing developmental state – most notably Chavismo in Venezuela and Morales-led Bolivia – have relied on global commodity markets (oil and gas in particular).
43. James M. Czank (2012) 'On the origins of species-being: Marx redefined'. *Rethinking Marxism 24* (2) p. 322.
44. Fraser, 2021, p. 96.
45. Goran Therborn (2014) 'New masses? Social bases of resistance'. *New Left Review* 85 p. 16.
46. While some western countries, most notably the US, did eventually send excess vaccines to non-western countries, even the notion that intellectual property rights might be waived was summarily dismissed.
47. Frantz Fanon. *Black skin, white masks* (New York: Grove Press, 1967) p. 37.

48. Karl Marx. *Critique of Hegel's philosophy of right* (Cambridge: Cambridge University Press, 1927).
49. Aasim Sajjad Akhtar (2016) 'Dreams of a secular republic: Elite alienation in post-Zia Pakistan'. *Journal of Contemporary Asia 46* (4) pp. 641–658.

EPILOGUE

1. Karl Marx (1843) Letter to Arnold Ruge.
2. Paul Mason. Postcapitalism: A guide to our future (London: Allen Lane, 2015); Yannis Varoufakis. *Another Now: dispatches from an alternative present* (London: Vintage Press, 2021).
3. Rob Wallace. *Dead epidemiologists: On the origins of COVID-19* (New York: Monthly Review Press, 2020).
4. Paulo Gerbaudo. *The digital party: Political organisation and online democracy* (London: Pluto Press, 2019).
5. Alastair Davidson (2008) 'The uses and abuses of Gramsci'. *Thesis Eleven* 95 (1) pp. 68–94.

Index

Thanks to our Patreon subscriber:

Ciaran Kane

Who has shown generosity and comradeship in support of our publishing.

Printed and bound by CPI Group (UK) Ltd, Croydon, CR0 4YY

17/09/2026

14964106-0001